SEW CUTE QUILTS AND GIFTS

30 lovely bags, quilts and accessories
to stitch, appliqué & embroider

ATSUKO MATSUYAMA

First published in Great Britain 2019

Search Press Limited
Wellwood, North Farm Road,
Tunbridge Wells, Kent TN2 3DR

Copyright © 2018 Boutique-sha, Inc.
ATSUKO MATSUYAMA HAPPY & LOVELY QUILT (LADY BOUTIQUE SERIES NO. 4637)
Originally published in Japanese language by Boutique-sha, Tokyo, Japan
English language rights, translation & production by Zakka Workshop,
a division of World Book Media LLC
Email: info@zakkaworkshop.com

English language rights, translation & production by Zakka Workshop
English Editors: Lindsay Fair
Translation: Ai Toyoda Jirka
Design: Debbie Berne

Suppliers
If you have any difficulty obtaining any of the materials and equipment mentioned in this book, please visit the Search Press website at www.searchpress.com

ISBN: 978-1-78221-762-6

Printed in China
10 9 8 7 6 5 4 3 2 1

CONTENTS

INTRODUCTION

If I had to pick two words to describe my work, I'd choose "happy" and "lovely."
As a young girl, I was fascinated by princesses and the beautiful clothes I'd see
them wear in books and movies. Inspired by their dresses, I'd collect ribbons,
lace, buttons, and sparkling beads in empty bottles and cookie tins. Sometimes,
I'd take them out just to look at them—they just made me feel so happy!

It's been over 30 years since I first started quilting, and I still can't get
enough of making pretty things. I just love adding special details and
embellishments to a project, and to me, there's never enough pink!

I hope that the projects in this book make you smile and say "how cute!" as you
flip through the pages. If this book makes you happy, then I will be happy!

—Atsuko Matsuyama

BAGS & POUCHES

This section includes a variety of uniquely shaped bags and pouches, all made with cute and colorful fabrics. These cheerful accessories are designed to brighten your day.

The rectangular shape allows you to store all sorts of items inside this pouch—it's great for travel and can be used inside a larger bag.

Add a ribbon tag for a special touch!

These simple patchwork pouches are excellent for beginners or those looking for a quick and easy project that can be made with scraps.

FLAT ZIPPERED POUCHES

MATERIALS

FOR THE WINDMILL POUCH

- Patchwork fabric: 12 assorted print scraps
- Neutral patchwork fabric: 8 in (20 cm) square of polka dot fabric
- Main fabric: 10 in (25 cm) square of blue floral print fabric
- Lining fabric: One fat quarter of print fabric
- Binding fabric: Two 1½ x 9¾ in (3.5 x 25 cm) bias strips
- Fusible fleece: 9¾ x 13¾ in (25 x 35 cm)
- 2½ in (6 cm) of ⅝ in (1.5 cm) wide grosgrain ribbon
- One 8 in (20 cm) zipper

FOR THE FLOWER POUCH

- Appliqué fabric: Assorted print scraps
- Appliqué background fabric: 6 in (15 cm) square of floral print fabric
- Patchwork fabric: 12 assorted prints
- Main fabric: 10 in (25 cm) square of pink floral print fabric
- Lining fabric: One fat quarter of print fabric
- Binding fabric: Two 1½ x 9¾ in (3.5 x 25 cm) bias strips
- Fusible fleece: 9¾ x 13¾ in (25 x 35 cm)
- 2½ in (6 cm) of ⅝ in (1.5 cm) wide grosgrain ribbon
- One 8 in (20 cm) zipper

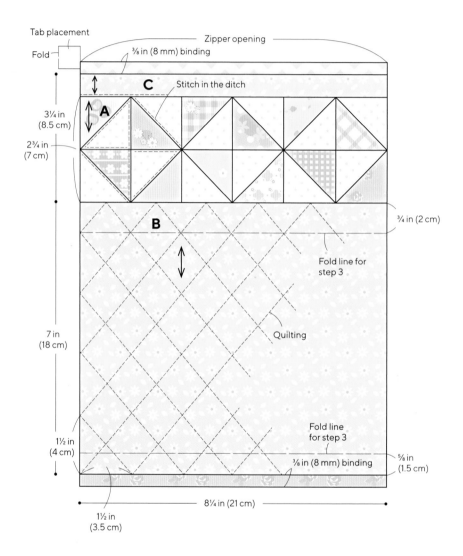

Tab placement

Fold

Zipper opening

⅜ in (8 mm) binding

C

Stitch in the ditch

A

3¼ in
(8.5 cm)

2¾ in
(7 cm)

B

¾ in (2 cm)

Fold line for
step 3

Quilting

7 in
(18 cm)

Fold line
for step 3

1½ in
(4 cm)

⅜ in (8 mm) binding

⅝ in
(1.5 cm)

8¼ in (21 cm)

1½ in
(3.5 cm)

CUTTING INSTRUCTIONS

Trace and cut out the templates on Pattern Sheet A. Use the templates to cut out the following pieces, adding ¼ in (6 mm) seam allowance.

PATCHWORK FABRIC

· 12 A pieces

NEUTRAL PATCHWORK FABRIC

· 12 A pieces

MAIN FABRIC

· 1 B piece

· 1 C piece

Sew using ¼ in (6 mm) seam allowance, unless otherwise noted.

Cut out the following pieces, which do not have templates, according to the dimensions listed below (these include seam allowance):

FUSIBLE FLEECE

· Fusible fleece: 8¾ x 11 in (22.2 x 27.7 cm)

LINING FABRIC

· Lining: 8¾ x 11 in (22.2 x 27.7 cm)

· Bias strips for side seams (cut 2): 1½ x 7 in (3.5 x 18 cm)

BINDING FABRIC

· Bias strips (cut 2): 1½ x 9¾ in (3.5 x 25 cm)

CONSTRUCTION STEPS

1. Sew the A pieces together in 12 sets of two. To achieve the windmill effect, you'll want to use one light fabric and one dark fabric for each set. Next, sew four sets together to make each block. Make three blocks, then sew together as shown in the project diagram on page 10.

2. Sew B to the lower edge of the assembled blocks and sew C to the upper edge. Adhere fusible fleece to the wrong side. Layer the lining underneath and quilt as noted on the template. Finally, bind the upper and lower edges of the pouch.

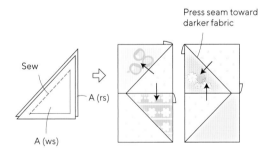

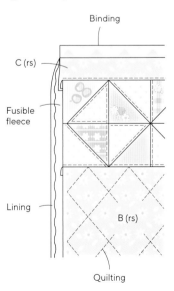

3. Fold the lower edge of the pouch up ⅝ in (1.5 cm) from the binding. Next, fold the upper edge down ¾ in (2 cm) beneath the patchwork blocks (these fold lines are noted in the project diagram on page 10). The bindings should be butted up next to each other and the lining should be facing up. Hand stitch the zipper to the bindings on the inside of the pouch. Make a tab from grosgrain ribbon and pin between the layers of the pouch at the end of the zipper.

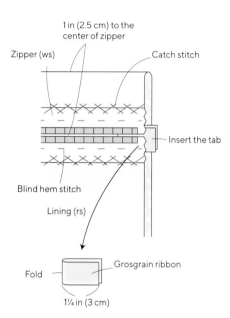

4. Make sure the zipper is partially open. Sew the pouch together along the sides. Bind the side seams.

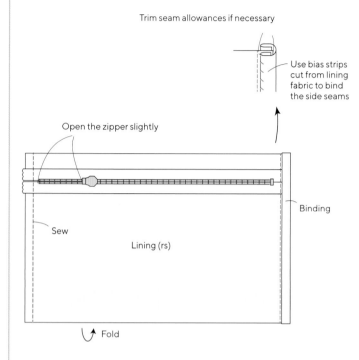

FINISHED DIAGRAM

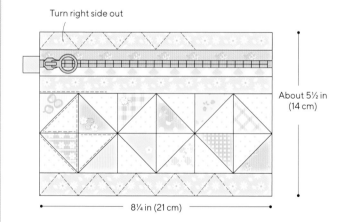

PROJECT DIAGRAM (FOR THE FLOWER POUCH)

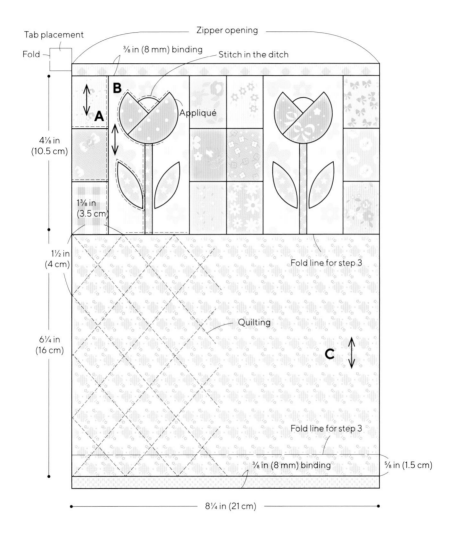

Tab placement

Fold

Zipper opening

⅜ in (8 mm) binding

Stitch in the ditch

B

A

Appliqué

4⅛ in (10.5 cm)

1⅜ in (3.5 cm)

1½ in (4 cm)

Fold line for step 3

6¼ in (16 cm)

Quilting

C

Fold line for step 3

⅜ in (8 mm) binding

⅝ in (1.5 cm)

8¼ in (21 cm)

CUTTING INSTRUCTIONS

Trace and cut out the templates on Pattern Sheet A. Use the templates to cut out the following pieces, adding ¼ in (6 mm) seam allowance.

APPLIQUÉ FABRIC
- 2 flower motifs

APPLIQUÉ BACKGROUND FABRIC
- 2 B pieces

PATCHWORK FABRIC
- 12 A pieces

Sew using ¼ in (6 mm) seam allowance, unless otherwise noted.

Cut out the following pieces, which do not have templates, according to the dimensions listed below (these include seam allowance):

MAIN FABRIC
- C: 8¾ x 6¾ in (22.2 x 17.2 cm)

FUSIBLE FLEECE
- Fusible fleece: 8¾ x 11 in (22.2 x 27.7 cm)

LINING FABRIC
- Lining: 8¾ x 11 in (22.2 x 27.7 cm)
- Bias strips for side seams (cut 2): 1½ x 7 in (3.5 x 18 cm)

BINDING FABRIC
- Bias strips (cut 2): 1½ x 9¾ in (3.5 x 25 cm)

CONSTRUCTION STEPS

1. Appliqué a flower motif to each B piece. Next, sew the A pieces together in four sets of three. Sew a set of A pieces to each side of a B piece to make each block. Sew the blocks together. Finally, sew C to the lower edge of the assembled blocks.

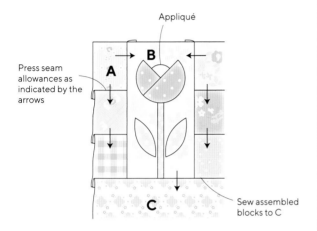

Appliqué

Press seam allowances as indicated by the arrows

Sew assembled blocks to C

2. Adhere fusible fleece to the wrong side. Layer the lining underneath and quilt as noted in the project diagram on page 13. Bind the upper and lower edges of the pouch.

3. Fold the lower edge of the pouch up ⅝ in (1.5 cm) from the binding. Next, fold the upper edge down at the seam beneath the patchwork blocks (these fold lines are noted in the project diagram on page 13). The bindings should be butted up next to each other and the lining should be facing up. Hand stitch the zipper to the bindings and make the tab, as shown in step 3 on page 12.

4. With the zipper partially open, sew the pouch together along the sides and bind the side seams, as shown in step 4 on page 12.

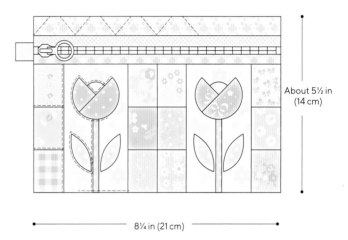

About 5½ in (14 cm)

8¼ in (21 cm)

This pouch features a magnetic snap closure to keep your belongings stored safely inside.

This sweet little pouch features a strawberry appliqué and a pretty lace ruffle on the flap. It's the perfect size for storing cosmetics.

STRAWBERRY RUFFLE POUCH

MATERIALS

- Appliqué fabric: Assorted print scraps
- Pouch fabric: One fat quarter of pink strawberry print fabric
- Flap fabric: 8 x 6 in (20 x 15 cm) of pink and white polka dot fabric
- Lining fabric: One fat quarter of print fabric
- Foundation fabric: ⅓ yd (0.3 m) of muslin
- Fusible fleece: 9¾ x 17¾ in (25 x 45 cm)
- 20 in (50 cm) of 1¼ in (3 cm) wide scalloped trim
- One ⅝ in (1.5 cm) magnetic snap
- Eight small red beads
- Two small clear beads
- #25 embroidery floss in green
- Two white flower-shaped lace appliqués
- Two green leaf-shaped appliqués

PROJECT DIAGRAM

FLAP (MAKE 1)

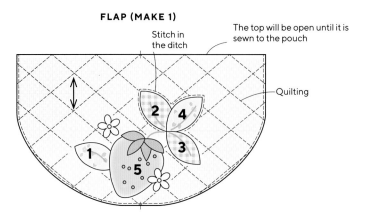

Stitch in the ditch

The top will be open until it is sewn to the pouch

Quilting

*Appliqué following numerical order noted above.

POUCH OUTSIDE (MAKE 1)

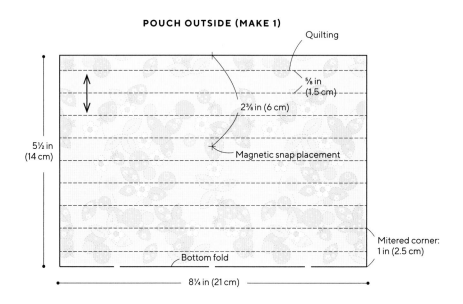

Quilting

⅝ in (1.5 cm)

2⅜ in (6 cm)

Magnetic snap placement

5½ in (14 cm)

Mitered corner: 1 in (2.5 cm)

Bottom fold

8¼ in (21 cm)

CUTTING INSTRUCTIONS

Trace and cut out the templates on Pattern Sheet A. Use the templates to cut out the following pieces, adding ¼ in (6 mm) seam allowance.

FLAP FABRIC, FUSIBLE FLEECE, FOUNDATION FABRIC, AND LINING

- 1 flap

Use the templates to cut out the following pieces, adding ⅛ in (3 mm) seam allowance.

APPLIQUÉ FABRIC

- Strawberry motif

Sew using ¼ in (6 mm) seam allowance, unless otherwise noted.

Cut out the following pieces, which do not have templates, according to the dimensions listed below (these include seam allowance):

POUCH FABRIC

- Pouch outside: 8¾ x 11½ in (22.2 x 29.2 cm)

FUSIBLE FLEECE

- Fusible fleece: 8¾ x 11½ in (22.2 x 29.2 cm)

FOUNDATION FABRIC

- Foundation fabric: 8¾ x 11½ in (22.2 x 29.2 cm)

LINING FABRIC

- Pouch lining: 8¾ x 11½ in (22.2 x 29.2 cm)

CONSTRUCTION STEPS

1. Appliqué and embroider the strawberry motif to the flap as noted on the template. Adhere fusible fleece to the wrong side of the flap. Layer the foundation fabric underneath and quilt as noted on the template.

Note: This bag is constructed with fusible fleece and a foundation fabric to provide support and structure. A separate lining will be added to hide these layers.

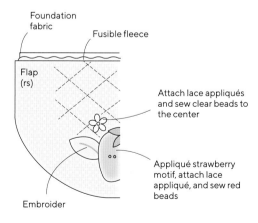

Foundation fabric

Fusible fleece

Flap (rs)

Attach lace appliqués and sew clear beads to the center

Appliqué strawberry motif, attach lace appliqué, and sew red beads

Embroider

2. Sew running stitch along the straight edge of the scalloped trim. Pull the thread tails to gather the trim into a ruffle and adjust as desired. With right sides together, align the straight edge of the trim with the flap from step 1. Sew together around the curve.

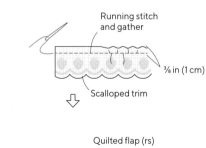

Running stitch and gather

⅜ in (1 cm)

Scalloped trim

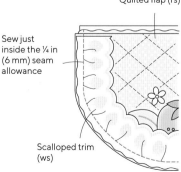

Quilted flap (rs)

Sew just inside the ¼ in (6 mm) seam allowance

Scalloped trim (ws)

3. With right sides together, align the flap lining with the flap so that the scalloped trim is sandwiched in between. Sew together around the curve, leaving the top open. Turn right side out. Topstitch the flap around the curve.

4. Adhere fusible fleece to the wrong side of the pouch outside. Layer the foundation fabric underneath and quilt as noted in the diagram on page 18. With right sides together, pin the center top of the flap to the center top of quilted pouch outside. Align the lining on top with the wrong side facing up and sew together along the top and bottom edges.

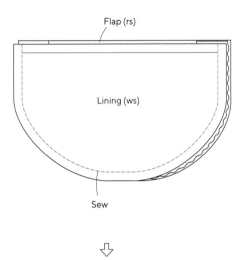

Flap (rs)

Lining (ws)

Sew

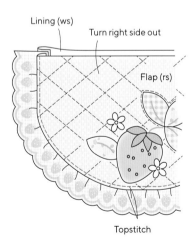

Lining (ws)

Turn right side out

Flap (rs)

Topstitch

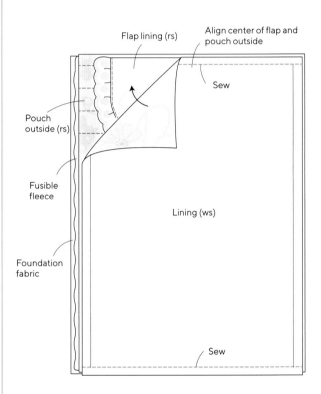

Flap lining (rs)

Align center of flap and pouch outside

Sew

Pouch outside (rs)

Fusible fleece

Lining (ws)

Foundation fabric

Sew

5. Align the pouch so that the seams from step 4 are centered. Press them open. Next, sew along the left and right edges, leaving an opening in the lining fabric. Press the seams open. Miter the corners of both the pouch outside and lining as shown below.

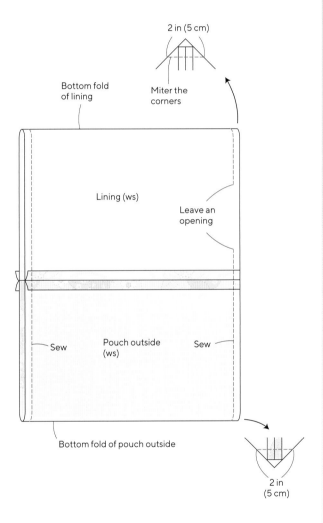

2 in (5 cm)

Bottom fold of lining

Miter the corners

Lining (ws)

Leave an opening

Sew

Pouch outside (ws)

Sew

Bottom fold of pouch outside

2 in (5 cm)

6. Turn right side out. Fold the opening seam allowances in and hand stitch closed. Tuck the lining inside the pouch.

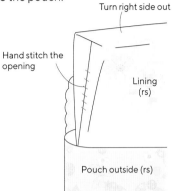

Turn right side out

Hand stitch the opening

Lining (rs)

Pouch outside (rs)

7. Topstitch around the top of the pouch to secure the lining in place. Sew the magnetic snap components to the pouch following the placement noted in the diagram on page 18 and on the template.

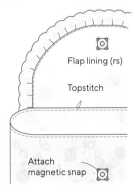

Flap lining (rs)

Topstitch

Attach magnetic snap

FINISHED DIAGRAM

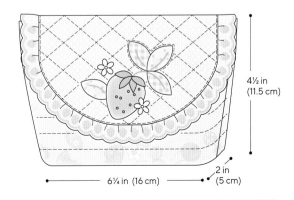

4½ in (11.5 cm)

6¼ in (16 cm)

2 in (5 cm)

These cute circle pouches are so colorful, I can almost taste the sweet and tangy flavor of fruit in my mouth! Use them for storing candy or small accessories.

ROUND FRUIT POUCHES

MATERIALS

FOR THE CHERRY POUCH

- Appliqué fabric: Assorted red and green scraps
- Patchwork fabric: 10 assorted prints
- Lining fabric: One fat eighth of print fabric
- Binding fabric: Two 1½ x 19¾ in (3.5 x 50 cm) bias strips
- Fusible fleece: 6 x 11¾ in (15 x 30 cm)
- 4 in (10 cm) of ⅜ in (8 mm) wide green rickrack
- One 8 in (20 cm) zipper with charm
- #25 embroidery floss in green

FOR THE STRAWBERRY POUCH

- Appliqué fabric: One pink scrap
- Patchwork fabric: 10 assorted prints
- Lining fabric: One fat eighth of print fabric
- Binding fabric: Two 1½ x 19¾ in (3.5 x 50 cm) bias strips
- Fusible fleece: 6 x 11¾ in (15 x 30 cm)

- Two green leaf-shaped lace appliqués
- One white flower-shaped lace appliqué
- One small bead
- One 8 in (20 cm) zipper with charm
- #25 embroidery floss in green

FOR THE APPLE POUCH

- Appliqué fabric: One green scrap
- Patchwork fabric: 10 assorted prints
- Lining fabric: One fat eighth of print fabric
- Binding fabric: Two 1½ x 19¾ in (3.5 x 50 cm) bias strips
- Fusible fleece: 6 x 11¾ in (15 x 30 cm)
- One green leaf-shaped lace appliqué
- One 8 in (20 cm) zipper with charm
- #25 embroidery floss in green and brown

PROJECT DIAGRAMS

CHERRY POUCH

FRONT (MAKE 1)

BACK (MAKE 1)

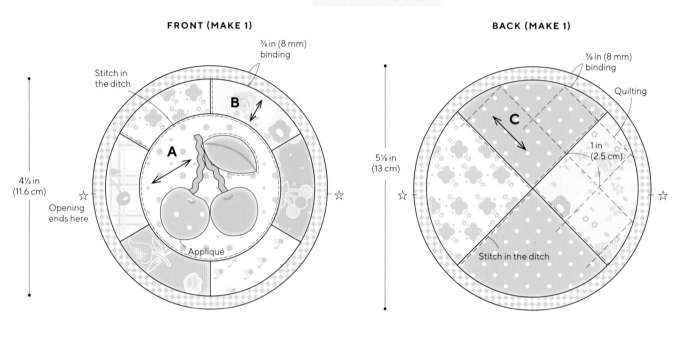

⅜ in (8 mm) binding

Stitch in the ditch

B

A

4½ in (11.6 cm)

Opening ends here

Appliqué

⅜ in (8 mm) binding

Quilting

C

1 in (2.5 cm)

5⅛ in (13 cm)

Stitch in the ditch

STRAWBERRY POUCH

FRONT (MAKE 1)

BACK (MAKE 1)

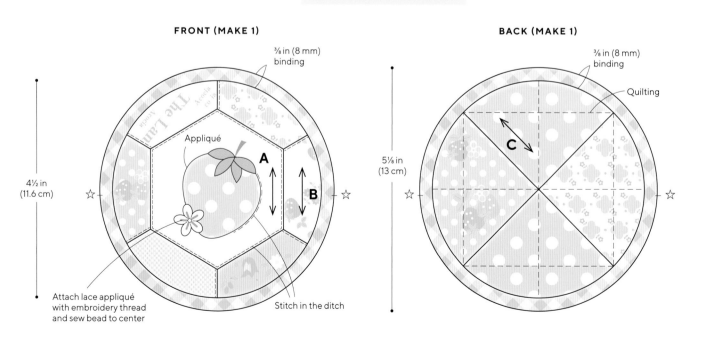

⅜ in (8 mm) binding

Appliqué

A

B

4½ in (11.6 cm)

Attach lace appliqué with embroidery thread and sew bead to center

Stitch in the ditch

⅜ in (8 mm) binding

Quilting

C

5⅛ in (13 cm)

APPLE POUCH

FRONT (MAKE 1)

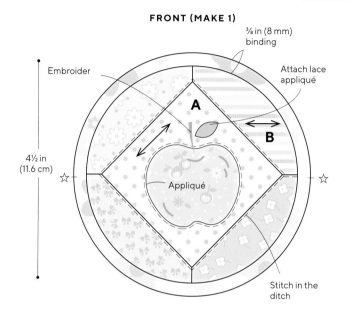

- ⅜ in (8 mm) binding
- Embroider
- Attach lace appliqué
- A
- B
- Appliqué
- 4½ in (11.6 cm)
- Stitch in the ditch

BACK (MAKE 1)

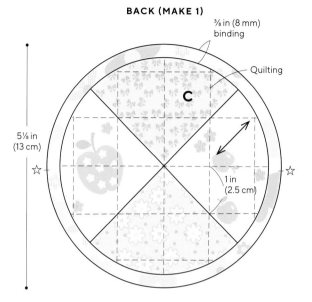

- ⅜ in (8 mm) binding
- Quilting
- C
- 5⅛ in (13 cm)
- 1 in (2.5 cm)

CUTTING INSTRUCTIONS (FOR ONE POUCH)

Trace and cut out the templates on Pattern Sheet A. Use the templates to cut out the following pieces, adding ¼ in (6 mm) seam allowance.

PATCHWORK FABRIC

- 1 A piece
- 6 B pieces for Cherry and Strawberry Pouches or 4 B pieces for Apple Pouch
- 4 C pieces

FUSIBLE FLEECE AND LINING FABRIC

- 2 circles

Sew using ¼ in (6 mm) seam allowance, unless otherwise noted.

Use the templates to cut out the following pieces, adding ⅛ in (3 mm) seam allowance.

APPLIQUÉ FABRIC

- Fruit appliqué motif

Cut out the following pieces, which do not have templates, according to the dimensions listed below (these include seam allowance):

BINDING FABRIC

- Bias strips (cut 2): 1½ x 19¾ in (3.5 x 50 cm)

CONSTRUCTION STEPS

1. Appliqué desired fruit motif to A, then embroider and embellish as noted on the template. Next, sew the B patchwork pieces to A to complete the front. Adhere fusible fleece to the wrong side of the front. Layer the lining underneath and quilt as noted on the template. Finally, sew the bias strip to the front, overlapping the ends as noted below.

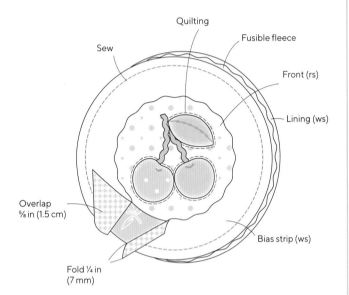

Quilting

Sew

Fusible fleece

Front (rs)

Lining (ws)

Overlap
⅝ in (1.5 cm)

Bias strip (ws)

Fold ¼ in
(7 mm)

2. Wrap the bias strip around the seam allowance and hand stitch to the lining.

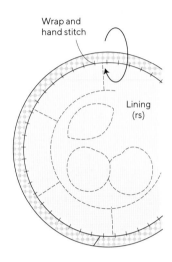

Wrap and
hand stitch

Lining
(rs)

3. Sew the C patchwork pieces together to make the back. Adhere fusible fleece to the wrong side, layer the lining underneath, and quilt as noted in the diagrams on pages 24–25. Bind following the same process used for the front.

4. Align the front and back with right sides together. Whipstitch the bindings together between the ☆ marks on the lower half of the pouch, as noted on the templates. Make sure to "backstitch" by adding more whipstitches ¼ in (5 mm) from the ☆ marks to reinforce the seam.

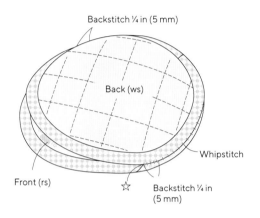

5. Hand stitch the zipper to the binding on the inside of the pouch (between the ☆ marks on the upper half of the pouch, as noted on the templates). The stitches should not be visible on the outside of the pouch.

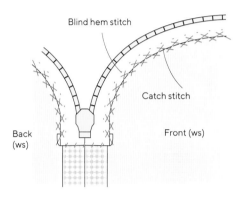

FINISHED DIAGRAM

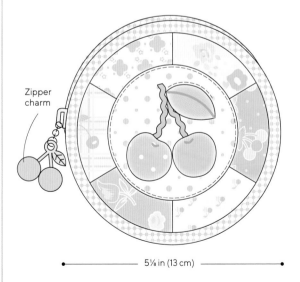

Rows of playful yoyo-shaped flowers bloom along the edges of this simple patchwork tote. I mixed both dots and checks for a casual look that is perfect for everyday use.

YOYO BUCKET BAG

MATERIALS

- Fabric #1: ¾ yd (0.7 m) of red and white polka dot fabric
- Fabric #2: ½ yd (0.5 m) of red and white gingham fabric
- Yoyo fabric: Assorted prints
- Lining fabric: ½ yd (0.5 m) of print fabric
- Foundation fabric: ⅓ yd (0.3 m) of muslin
- Fusible fleece: 35½ x 9¾ in (90 x 25 cm)
- 28 in (70 cm) of ⅝ in (1.5 cm) wide red rickrack
- One ⅝ in (1.5 cm) magnetic snap

PROJECT DIAGRAM

BAG OUTSIDES (MAKE 2)

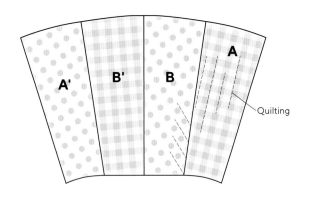

LININGS (MAKE 2)

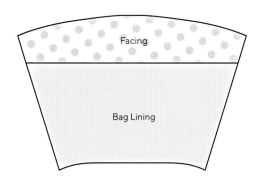

BOTTOM (MAKE 1)

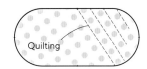

HANDLES (MAKE 2 OF EACH)

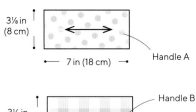

CUTTING INSTRUCTIONS

Trace and cut out the templates on Pattern Sheet A. Use the templates to cut out the following pieces, adding ¼ in (6 mm) seam allowance.

FABRIC #1
- 2 A' pieces
- 2 B pieces
- 1 bottom
- 2 facings

FABRIC #2
- 2 A pieces
- 2 B' pieces

FUSIBLE FLEECE
- 2 bag outsides
- 1 bottom

FOUNDATION FABRIC
- 2 bag outsides
- 1 bottom

LINING FABRIC
- 1 bottom lining
- 2 bag linings

Use the template to cut out the following pieces, but do not add seam allowance:

YOYO FABRIC
- About 40 yoyos

Sew using ¼ in (6 mm) seam allowance, unless otherwise noted.

Cut out the following pieces, which do not have templates, according to the dimensions listed below (these include seam allowance):

FABRIC #1
- Handle A (cut 2): 3⅛ x 7 in (8 x 18 cm)

FABRIC #2
- Handle B (cut 2): 3⅛ x 7 in (8 x 18 cm)

CONSTRUCTION STEPS

1. Sew pieces A', B', B, and A together to make each bag outside. Adhere fusible fleece to the wrong side of each assembled bag outside. Layer the foundation fabric underneath. Quilt as noted on the template.

Note: This bag is constructed with fusible fleece and a foundation fabric to provide support and structure. A separate lining will be added to hide these layers.

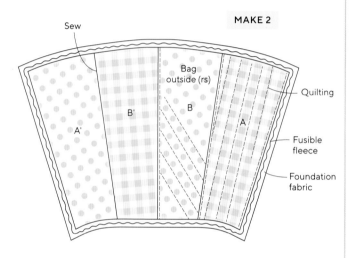

MAKE 2

Sew

Bag outside (rs)

Quilting

Fusible fleece

Foundation fabric

A'   B'   B   A

2. Align the two bag outsides with right sides together. Sew together along the sides. Press the seam allowances open.

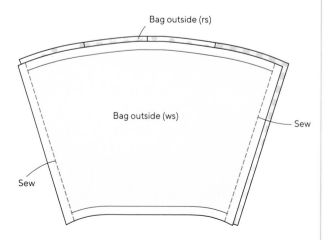

Bag outside (rs)

Bag outside (ws)

Sew

Sew

3. Adhere fusible fleece to the wrong side of the bottom. Layer the foundation fabric underneath. Quilt as noted on the template.

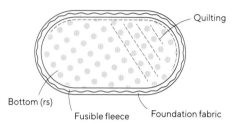

Quilting

Bottom (rs)

Fusible fleece   Foundation fabric

4. Sew the bottom to the bag with right sides together.

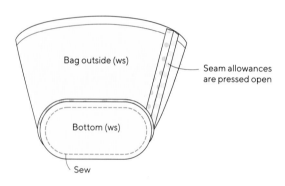

Bag outside (ws)

Seam allowances are pressed open

Bottom (ws)

Sew

5. To make the handles, sew each handle A piece to a handle B piece with right sides together. Press open. Fold and press each long edge ⅜ in (1 cm) to the wrong side, then fold each handle in half. Topstitch close to the long edges, then topstitch a piece of rickrack along the center of each handle.

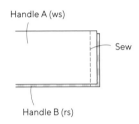

Handle A (ws)

Sew

Handle B (rs)

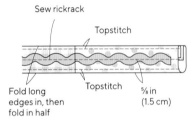

Sew rickrack

Topstitch

Topstitch

Fold long edges in, then fold in half

⅝ in (1.5 cm)

6. Sew each handle to the bag following the placement noted on the template. Make sure to align the handles with the rickrack facing down.

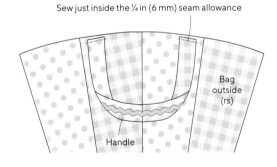

Sew just inside the ¼ in (6 mm) seam allowance

Bag outside (rs)

Handle

7. With right sides together, sew a facing to each bag lining. Align the two assembled bag linings with right sides together. Sew together along the sides, leaving a 4 in (10 cm) opening in one side. Press the seam allowances open. Sew the bottom lining to the bag lining with right sides together.

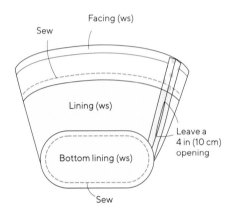

Facing (ws)

Sew

Lining (ws)

Leave a 4 in (10 cm) opening

Bottom lining (ws)

Sew

8. Insert the assembled lining into the bag with right sides together. Sew the two together around the top.

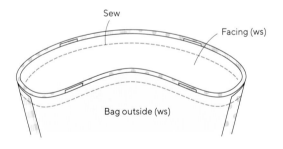

Sew

Facing (ws)

Bag outside (ws)

9. Turn right side out. Fold the opening seam allowances in and hand stitch closed. Tuck the lining inside the bag. Blind hem stitch around the top of the bag to secure the lining in place.

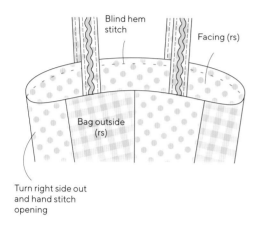

Blind hem stitch

Facing (rs)

Bag outside (rs)

Turn right side out and hand stitch opening

10. Use the template to make the yoyos as shown below. You'll need approximately 40 yoyos.

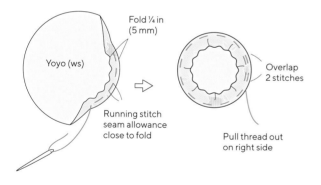

Fold ¼ in (5 mm)

Yoyo (ws)

Running stitch seam allowance close to fold

Overlap 2 stitches

Pull thread out on right side

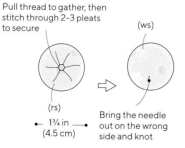

Pull thread to gather, then stitch through 2–3 pleats to secure

(ws)

(rs)

1¾ in (4.5 cm)

Bring the needle out on the wrong side and knot

11. Hand stitch the yoyos to the bag in two rounds of 20 yoyos each.

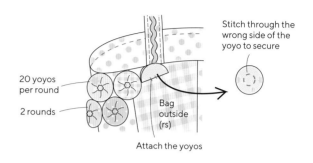

Stitch through the wrong side of the yoyo to secure

20 yoyos per round

2 rounds

Bag outside (rs)

Attach the yoyos

FINISHED DIAGRAM

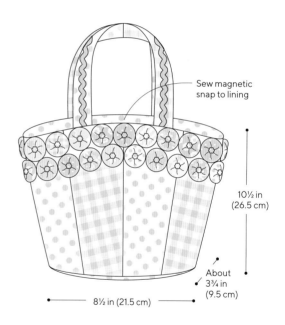

Sew magnetic snap to lining

10½ in (26.5 cm)

About 3¾ in (9.5 cm)

8½ in (21.5 cm)

Don't forget to sew yoyos to the bottom of the pouch too!

This cute round pouch is almost completely covered in yoyos, and reminds me of a field of flowers in bloom. Have fun experimenting with the balance of color and pattern as you determine yoyo placement.

BLOOMING YOYO POUCH

MATERIALS

- Yoyo fabric: Assorted print scraps
- Covered button fabric: Assorted print scraps
- Main fabric: ¼ yd (0.3 m) of pink print fabric
- Lining fabric: ½ yd (0.5 m) of print fabric
- Foundation fabric: ⅓ yd (0.3 m) of muslin
- Fusible fleece: 21¾ x 11¾ in (55 x 30 cm)
- 51¼ in (130 cm) of ⅛ in (3 mm) thick pink waxed cord
- Four ¾ in (2 cm) cover buttons
- 22 white flower-shaped lace appliqués
- Pearl cotton #8 in red

PROJECT DIAGRAM

POUCH OUTSIDES (MAKE 2)

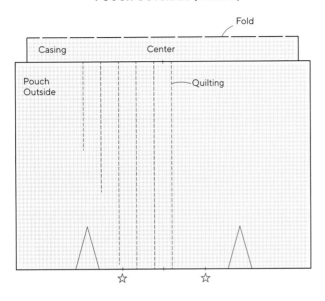

Fold

Casing   Center

Pouch
Outside

Quilting

BOTTOM (MAKE 1)

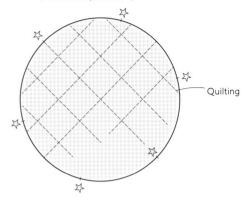

Quilting

YOYOS (MAKE 55)

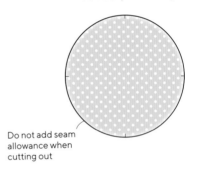

Do not add seam
allowance when
cutting out

COVERED BUTTONS (MAKE 4)

Do not add seam
allowance when
cutting out

Sew using
¼ in (6 mm) seam
allowance, unless
otherwise noted.

CUTTING INSTRUCTIONS

Trace and cut out the templates on Pattern Sheet A. Use the templates to cut out the following pieces, adding ¼ in (6 mm) seam allowance.

MAIN FABRIC
- 2 pouch outsides
- 1 bottom
- 4 casings (cut on fold)

FUSIBLE FLEECE, FOUNDATION FABRIC, AND LINING FABRIC
- 2 pouch outsides
- 1 bottom

Use the templates to cut out the following pieces, but do not add seam allowance:

YOYO FABRIC
- About 55 yoyos

COVERED BUTTON FABRIC
- 4 covered button circles

CONSTRUCTION STEPS

1. Adhere fusible fleece to the wrong side of each pouch outside. Layer the foundation fabric underneath. Quilt as noted on the template.

Note: This bag is constructed with fusible fleece and a foundation fabric to provide support and structure. A separate lining will be added to hide these layers.

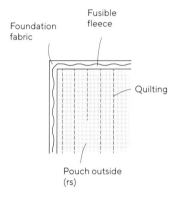

2. Sew the darts on each pouch outside (refer to the template for placement). Align each pouch outside with right sides together and sew together along the sides. Press the seam allowances open.

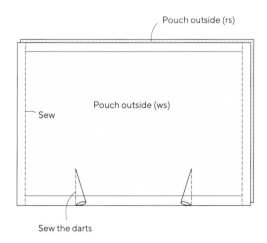

3. Adhere fusible fleece to the wrong side of the bottom. Layer the foundation fabric underneath. Quilt as noted in the template. Sew the bottom to the pouch with right sides together.

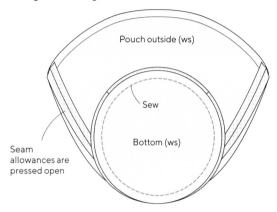

4. Use the template to make the yoyos as shown in the guide on page 39. You'll need approximately 55 yoyos.

5. Hand stitch the yoyos to the pouch in four rounds of 12 yoyos each. Use pearl cotton #8 in red to embroider crosses connecting the yoyos.

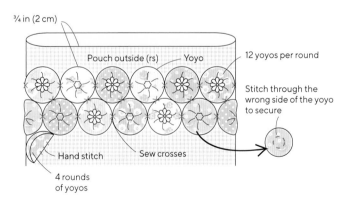

6. Hand stitch seven yoyos to the bottom of the pouch. Use pearl cotton #8 in red to embroider crosses connecting the yoyos.

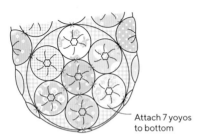

Attach 7 yoyos to bottom

7. Align two casing pieces with right sides together. Sew together along the sides. Turn right side out. Repeat to make another casing.

MAKE 2

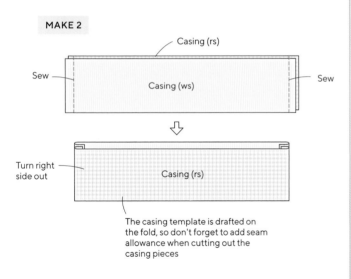

Casing (rs)

Sew

Casing (ws)

Sew

Turn right side out

Casing (rs)

The casing template is drafted on the fold, so don't forget to add seam allowance when cutting out the casing pieces

8. Fold each casing in half. Align the raw edges of each casing with the top of the pouch. Sew, stitching just inside the seam allowance.

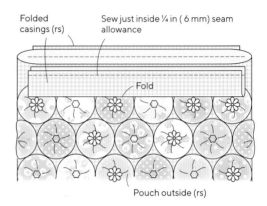

Folded casings (rs)

Sew just inside ¼ in (6 mm) seam allowance

Fold

Pouch outside (rs)

9. Align the two pouch linings with right sides together. Sew together along the sides. Press the seam allowances open. Sew the bottom lining to the pouch lining with right sides together.

10. Insert the lining into the pouch with wrong sides together. Fold the seam allowances in on both the lining and pouch, then sew around the top to secure the lining in place. Make sure to fold the casings up and out of the way while sewing. **Note:** You may want to hand stitch the casings to the lining on the inside of the pouch in order to keep them in an upright position.

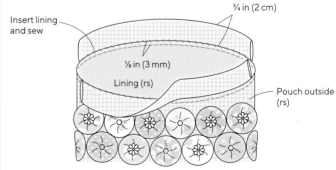

Insert lining and sew

¾ in (2 cm)

⅛ in (3 mm)

Lining (rs)

Pouch outside (rs)

11. Insert a 25½ in (65 cm) long cord through each casing. Sew the ends together. Make two covered buttons, then sew together to cover the cord ends. Repeat, inserting the remaining length of cord through the casings in the opposite direction.

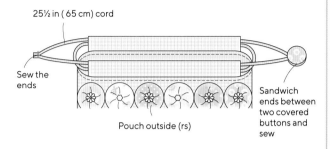

25½ in (65 cm) cord

Sew the ends

Pouch outside (rs)

Sandwich ends between two covered buttons and sew

FINISHED DIAGRAM

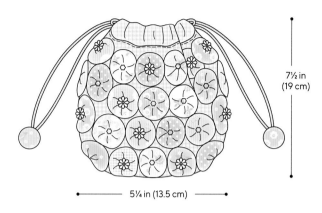

7½ in (19 cm)

5¼ in (13.5 cm)

HOW TO MAKE THE YOYOS

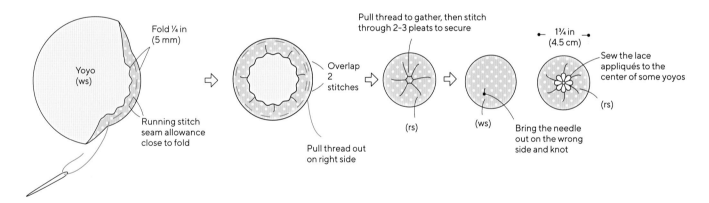

Fold ¼ in (5 mm)

Yoyo (ws)

Running stitch seam allowance close to fold

Overlap 2 stitches

Pull thread out on right side

Pull thread to gather, then stitch through 2-3 pleats to secure

(rs)

(ws)

Bring the needle out on the wrong side and knot

1¾ in (4.5 cm)

Sew the lace appliqués to the center of some yoyos

(rs)

HOW TO MAKE A COVERED BUTTON

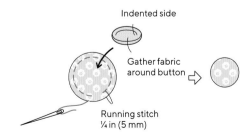

Indented side

Gather fabric around button

Running stitch ¼ in (5 mm)

Colorful floral appliqués dance around the perimeter of the elegant round bag. I chose a neutral background fabric so the flowers would really pop, then added braided fabric handles for a pretty accent.

DANCING FLOWERS PURSE

MATERIALS

- Appliqué fabric: Assorted print scraps
- Main fabric: ¾ yd (0.6 m) of cotton/polyester blend grosgrain dot fabric
- Accent fabric: One fat eighth of red floral print fabric
- Lining fabric: ¾ yd (0.6 m) of print fabric
- Foundation fabric: ¾ yd (0.6 m) of muslin
- Fusible fleece: 19¾ x 21¾ in (50 x 55 cm)
- #25 embroidery floss in pink, purple, and green

PROJECT DIAGRAM

FACINGS (MAKE 2)

Mountain fold

Fold

HANDLE PIECES (MAKE 6 TOTAL)

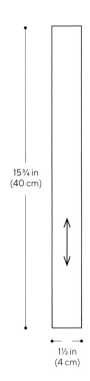

15¾ in
(40 cm)

1½ in
(4 cm)

FRONT & BACK (MAKE 1 OF EACH)

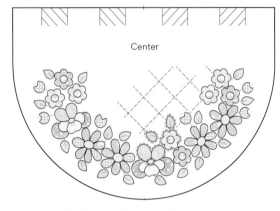

Center

* Appliqué motif appears on bag front only.

CUTTING INSTRUCTIONS

Trace and cut out the templates on Pattern Sheet B. Use the templates to cut out the following pieces, adding ¼ in (6 mm) seam allowance.

MAIN FABRIC

- 1 front
- 1 back
- 2 facings

FUSIBLE FLEECE, FOUNDATION FABRIC, AND LINING FABRIC

- 1 front
- 1 back

Use the templates to cut out the following pieces, adding ⅛ in (3 mm) seam allowance.

APPLIQUÉ FABRIC

- Floral appliqué motif

Sew using ¼ in (6 mm) seam allowance, unless otherwise noted.

Cut out the following pieces, which do not have templates, according to the dimensions listed below (these include seam allowance):

MAIN FABRIC

- Handle pieces (cut 4): 1½ x 15¾ in (4 x 40 cm)

ACCENT FABRIC

- Handle pieces (cut 2): 1½ x 15¾ in (4 x 40 cm)

CONSTRUCTION STEPS

1. Appliqué and embroider the floral motif to the front as noted on the template. Adhere fusible fleece to the wrong side of the front. Layer the foundation fabric underneath and quilt as noted on the template.

Note: This bag is constructed with fusible fleece and a foundation fabric to provide support and structure. A separate lining will be added to hide these layers.

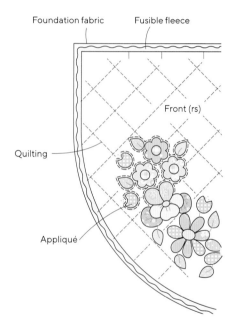

2. Adhere fusible fleece to the wrong side of the back. Layer the foundation fabric underneath and quilt as desired. Next, align the front and back with right sides together and sew around the curve, leaving the top open.

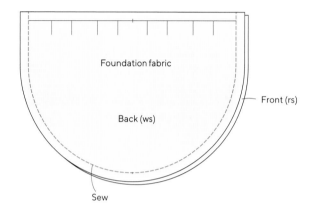

3. Turn the bag right side out. Fold the pleats as noted on the template. Baste in place, stitching inside the seam allowance.

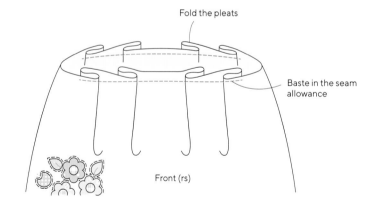

4. With right sides together, sew the lining pieces together around the curve. Turn right side out. Follow the same process used in step 3 to fold and baste the pleats.

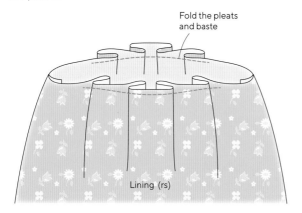

Fold the pleats and baste

Lining (rs)

5. Fold and press the long edges of each handle piece in to the center. Next, fold each handle piece in half and press. Topstitch close to each long edge. To make each handle, work a three-strand braid using two main fabric pieces and one accent fabric piece until the handle measures about 12¾ in (32 cm). Baste about ¼ in (5 mm) from each end to secure the braid in place.

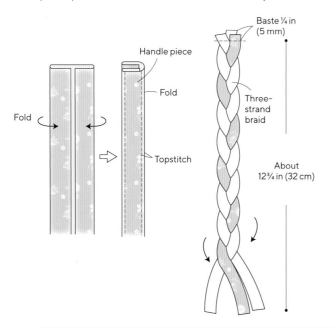

Fold

Handle piece

Fold

Topstitch

Baste ¼ in (5 mm)

Three-strand braid

About 12¾ in (32 cm)

6. Baste the handles to the bag, stitching just inside the ¼ in (6 mm) seam allowance. The handles should be aligned with the bag just inside the outer pleats.

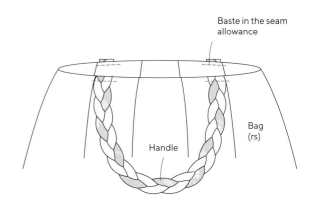

Baste in the seam allowance

Handle

Bag (rs)

7. Align the two facings with right sides together. Sew together along the short ends. Press the seam allowances open.

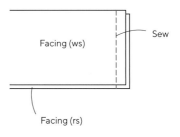

Facing (ws)

Sew

Facing (rs)

8. Insert the lining inside the bag with wrong sides together. Next, align the facing with the right side of the bag. Sew together around the top of the bag.

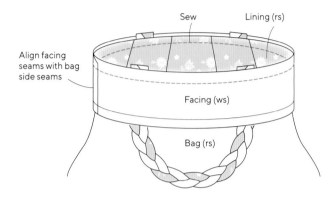

Sew   Lining (rs)

Align facing seams with bag side seams

Facing (ws)

Bag (rs)

9. Fold half of the facing to the inside of the bag. Fold the facing seam allowance under and hand stitch to the lining. Use a few hand stitches to secure the handles to the facing in an upright position.

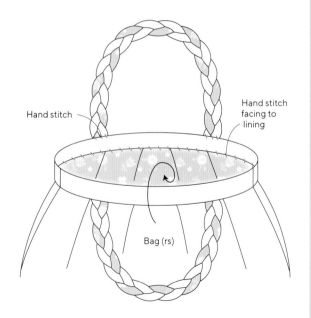

Hand stitch

Hand stitch facing to lining

Bag (rs)

FINISHED DIAGRAM

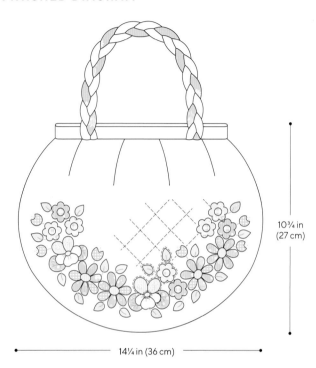

10¾ in (27 cm)

14¼ in (36 cm)

This patchwork purse features a variety of soft-toned print fabrics and is embellished with floral embroidery. The straps are the perfect length for wearing over the shoulder.

PASTEL HEXAGON PURSE

MATERIALS

- Patchwork fabric: Assorted print scraps
- Main fabric: ½ yd (0.5 m) of pink cotton/polyester blend grosgrain dot fabric
- Lining fabric: ¾ yd (0.7 m) of print fabric
- Foundation fabric: ¾ yd (0.7 m) of muslin
- Fusible fleece: 19¾ x 27¾ in (50 x 70 cm)
- #25 embroidery floss in pink, light pink, yellow green, green, yellow, light blue, purple, and light purple

PROJECT DIAGRAM

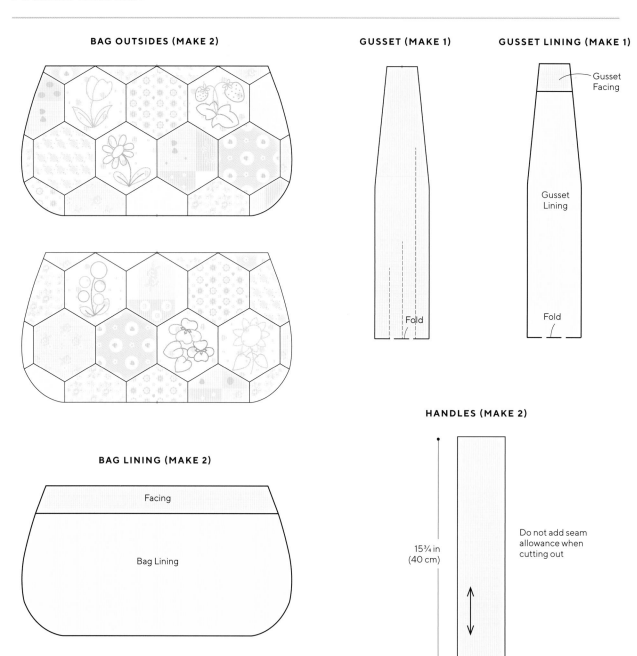

BAG OUTSIDES (MAKE 2)

GUSSET (MAKE 1)

Fold

GUSSET LINING (MAKE 1)

Gusset Facing

Gusset Lining

Fold

BAG LINING (MAKE 2)

Facing

Bag Lining

HANDLES (MAKE 2)

15¾ in (40 cm)

Do not add seam allowance when cutting out

3⅛ in (8 cm)

CUTTING INSTRUCTIONS

Trace and cut out the templates on Pattern Sheet B. Use the templates to cut out the following pieces, adding ¼ in (6 mm) seam allowance.

PATCHWORK FABRIC
- 40 hexagons

FUSIBLE FLEECE AND FOUNDATION FABRIC
- 2 bag outsides
- 1 gusset

MAIN FABRIC
- 1 gusset
- 2 bag facings
- 2 gusset facings

LINING FABRIC
- 2 bag linings
- 1 gusset lining

Cut out the following pieces, which do not have templates, according to the dimensions listed below (these include seam allowance):

FABRIC A
- Handles (cut 2): 3⅛ x 15¾ in (8 x 40 cm)

Sew using ¼ in (6 mm) seam allowance, unless otherwise noted.

CONSTRUCTION STEPS

1. Sew the hexagons together to make two bag outsides. Embroider using the templates on the pattern sheet. **Note:** These instructions use traditional hand piecing to assemble the hexagons. You can also use English paper piecing to assemble the hexagons, then trim into shape using the bag outside template (just don't forget to add seam allowance before cutting!).

2. Adhere fusible fleece to the wrong side of each bag outside. Layer the foundation fabric underneath. Quilt as noted on the template.

Note: This bag is constructed with fusible fleece and a foundation fabric to provide support and structure. A separate lining will be added to hide these layers.

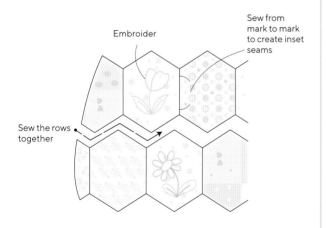

Embroider

Sew from mark to mark to create inset seams

Sew the rows together

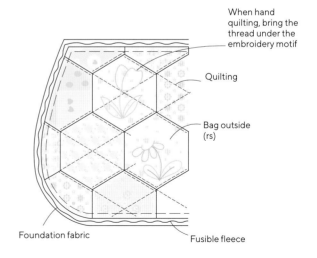

When hand quilting, bring the thread under the embroidery motif

Quilting

Bag outside (rs)

Foundation fabric

Fusible fleece

3. Adhere fusible fleece to the wrong side of the gusset. Layer the foundation fabric underneath. Quilt as noted on the template.

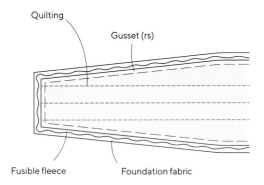

5. With right sides together, sew a facing to each bag lining. With right sides together, sew a gusset facing to each short end of the gusset lining.

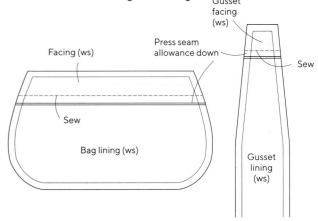

4. With right sides together, sew the long edges of the gusset to the two bag outsides.

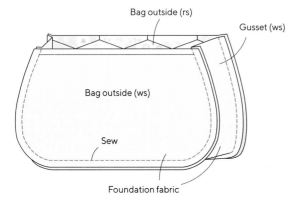

6. With right sides together, sew the long edges of the gusset lining to the two bag linings, leaving a 4 in (10 cm) opening at the bottom of one of the bag linings.

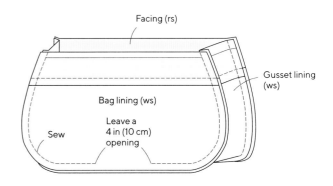

7. Fold and press the long edges of each handle in ¾ in (2 cm) to the wrong side. Fold each handle in half and topstitch close to the long edges.

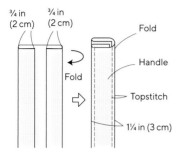

8. Sew each handle to the bag following the placement noted on the template.

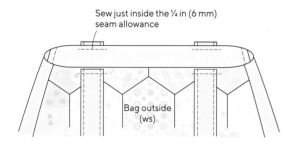

9. Insert the assembled lining into the bag with right sides together. Sew the two together around the top.

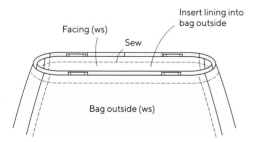

10. Turn right side out. Fold the opening seam allowances in and hand stitch closed. Tuck the lining inside the bag. Blind hem stitch around the top of the bag to secure the lining in place.

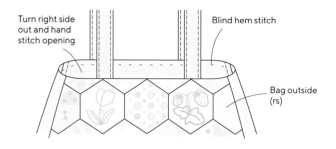

FINISHED DIAGRAM

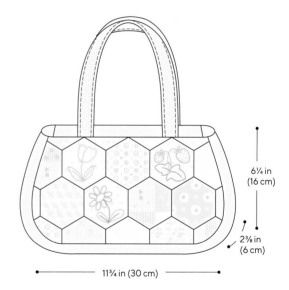

The flap features a small bow for added cuteness!

These pouches are great for organizing cosmetics or small sewing projects.

Simply change the size of the hexagons to make the three different sizes of these precious pouches. Use bright, bold prints for a scrappy, cheerful look.

HEXAGON POUCH TRIO

MATERIALS

FOR THE LARGE POUCH
- Patchwork fabric: 16 assorted print scraps, measuring 4 in (10 cm) square each
- Bow fabric: 6 x 9¾ in (15 x 25 cm) of print fabric
- Lining fabric: One fat quarter of print fabric
- Fusible fleece: 19¾ x 13¾ in (50 x 35 cm)
- One ⅝ in (1.5 cm) diameter magnetic snap

FOR THE MEDIUM POUCH
- Patchwork fabric: 16 assorted print scraps, measuring 3⅛ in (8 cm) square each
- Bow fabric: 4 x 8 in (10 x 20 cm) of print fabric
- Lining fabric: One fat quarter of print fabric
- Fusible fleece: 15¾ x 11¾ in (40 x 30 cm)
- One ⅜ in (1 cm) diameter magnetic snap

FOR THE SMALL POUCH
- Patchwork fabric: 16 assorted print scraps, measuring 2⅜ in (6 cm) square each
- Bow fabric: 3⅛ x 8 in (8 x 20 cm) of print fabric
- Lining fabric: One fat eighth of print fabric
- Fusible fleece: 11¾ x 8 in (30 x 20 cm)
- One ⅜ in (1 cm) diameter magnetic snap

PROJECT DIAGRAM

POUCH TOP (MAKE 1)

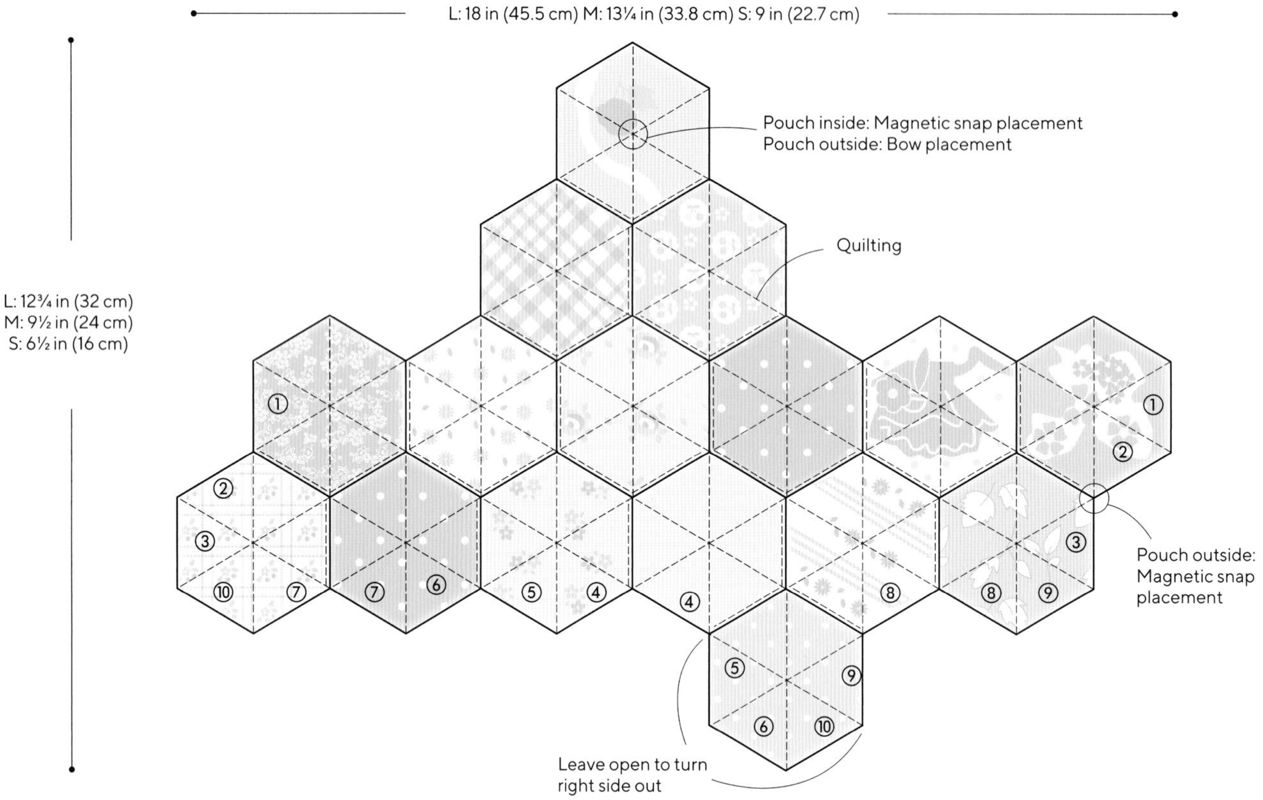

L: 18 in (45.5 cm) M: 13¼ in (33.8 cm) S: 9 in (22.7 cm)

L: 12¾ in (32 cm)
M: 9½ in (24 cm)
S: 6½ in (16 cm)

Pouch inside: Magnetic snap placement
Pouch outside: Bow placement

Quilting

Pouch outside: Magnetic snap placement

Leave open to turn right side out

CUTTING INSTRUCTIONS

Trace and cut out the templates on Pattern Sheet A. Use the templates to cut out the following pieces, adding ¼ in (6 mm) seam allowance.

PATCHWORK FABRIC

- 16 hexagons

BOW FABRIC

- 2 A pieces
- 2 B pieces
- 2 center pieces

You'll use the assembled pouch top as a template to cut the lining and fusible fleece in steps 1 and 2.

Sew using ¼ in (6 mm) seam allowance, unless otherwise noted.

CONSTRUCTION STEPS

1. Sew the hexagons together to make the pouch top. Use the assembled pouch top as a template to cut out the fusible fleece in the same size and shape. Adhere the fusible fleece to the wrong side of the pouch top.

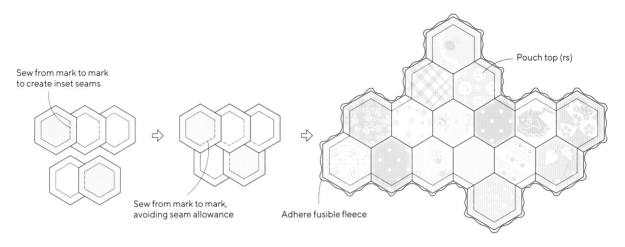

Sew from mark to mark to create inset seams

Sew from mark to mark, avoiding seam allowance

Adhere fusible fleece

Pouch top (rs)

2. Use the pouch top from step 1 as a template to cut out a lining in the same size and shape. Align the pouch top and lining with right sides together. Sew together around the outline, leaving one hexagon open along three sides. Trim the excess fusible fleece from the seam allowance and make small clips into the seam allowance at the interior corners.

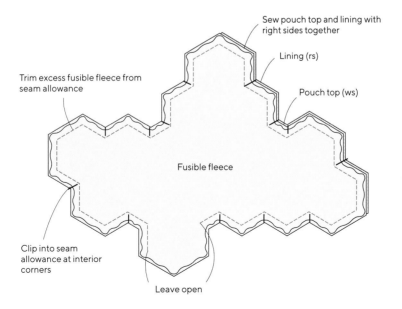

Trim excess fusible fleece from seam allowance

Sew pouch top and lining with right sides together

Lining (rs)

Pouch top (ws)

Fusible fleece

Clip into seam allowance at interior corners

Leave open

3. Turn right side out. Fold the opening seam allowances in and hand stitch closed. Quilt as noted below.
Note: For the small pouch, quilt along the perimeter of the hexagons only. Do not quilt the intersecting diagonal lines.

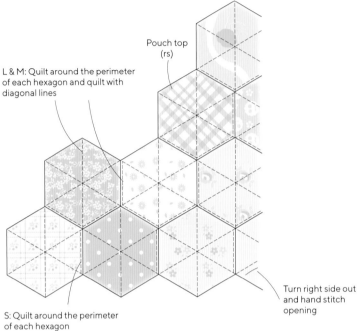

Pouch top (rs)

L & M: Quilt around the perimeter of each hexagon and quilt with diagonal lines

Turn right side out and hand stitch opening

S: Quilt around the perimeter of each hexagon

4. Fold the pouch into shape by aligning corresponding numbers as noted in the diagram on page 54. Whipstitch the pouch together, stitching through the top layer of fabric only (do not stitch through the lining).

Pouch top (rs)

① ② Lining (rs)

Align corresponding numbers and whipstitch

5. Sew the magnetic snap components to the pouch following the placement noted in the diagram on page 54.

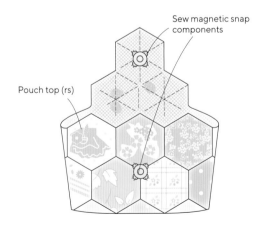

Sew magnetic snap components

Pouch top (rs)

6. Make the bow as shown below, then sew it to the pouch outside following the placement noted in the diagram on page 54.

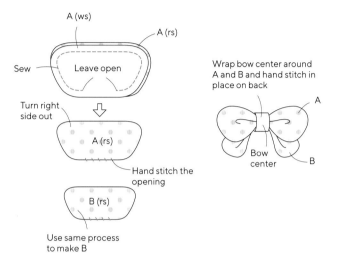

FINISHED DIAGRAM

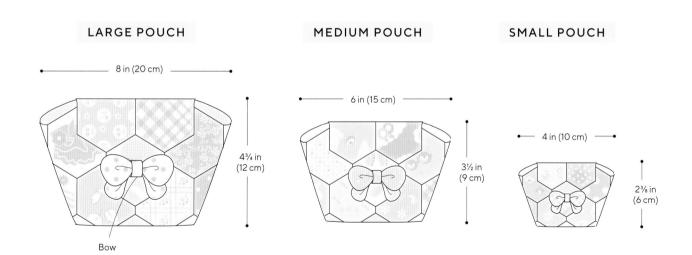

LARGE POUCH

MEDIUM POUCH

SMALL POUCH

A metal purse clasp provides this simple patchwork pouch with structure and style. The clutch is the perfect size for holding your essentials.

This sweet little pouch is extremely versatile—
use it as a makeup case inside a larger bag or as a
clutch for a special evening out on the town.

LAVENDER CLUTCH

MATERIALS

- Patchwork fabric: Eight assorted print scraps
- Lining fabric: One fat quarter of print fabric
- Foundation fabric: ½ yd (0.5 m) of muslin
- Lightweight fusible fleece: 13¾ x 13¾ in (35 x 35 cm)
- 27½ in (70 cm) of ⅜ in (1 cm) wide flower-shaped lace trim
- One 7 x 2½ in (18 x 6.5 cm) sew-in metal clasp
- #25 embroidery floss in purple and light purple
- Pearl cotton #8 in variegated purple

PROJECT DIAGRAM

POUCH OUTSIDES (MAKE 2)

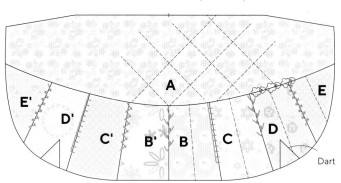

CUTTING INSTRUCTIONS

Trace and cut out the templates on Pattern Sheet B. Use the templates to cut out the following pieces, adding ¼ in (6 mm) seam allowance.

FUSIBLE FLEECE, FOUNDATION FABRIC, AND LINING FABRIC

- 2 pouch outsides

PATCHWORK FABRIC

- 2 A pieces
- 2 B pieces
- 2 B' pieces
- 2 C pieces
- 2 C' pieces
- 2 D pieces
- 2 D' pieces
- 2 E pieces
- 2 E' pieces

Sew using ¼ in (6 mm) seam allowance, unless otherwise noted.

CONSTRUCTION STEPS

1. Sew pieces A–E together to make two pouch outsides. Adhere fusible fleece to the wrong side of each pouch outside. Layer the foundation fabric underneath and quilt as noted on the template. Embroider and sew the lace as noted on the template.

Note: This bag is constructed with fusible fleece and a foundation fabric to provide support and structure. A separate lining will be added to hide these layers.

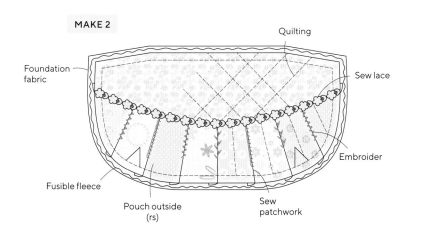

2. Sew the darts on each pouch outside (refer to the template for placement). Align each pouch outside with right sides together and sew, leaving the top open.

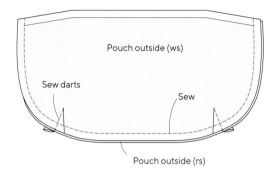

3. Repeat step 2 using the two lining pieces.

4. Insert the lining into the pouch with right sides together. Sew together around the top, leaving an opening.

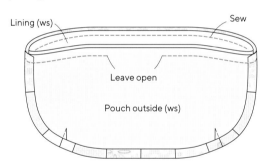

5. Turn right side out. Fold the opening seam allowances in and hand stitch closed. Tuck the lining into the pouch.

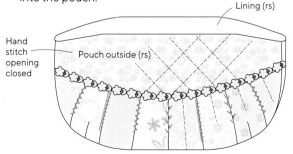

6. Insert the pouch into the metal clasp. Baste the pouch to the clasp in several spots to temporarily hold in place (refer to step 8 on page 67). Use pearl cotton #8 to backstitch the pouch to the clasp.

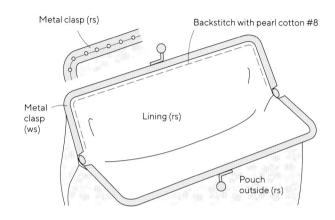

FINISHED DIAGRAM

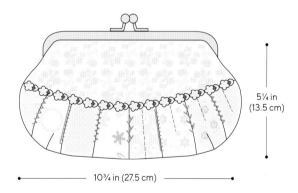

This adorable pouch features a rounded silhouette, but is actually composed of scrappy rectangles. The patchwork is then embellished with a variety of beads and decorative embroidery stitches for a cheerful look.

PUFFY POUCH

MATERIALS

- Patchwork fabric: Six assorted print scraps
- Gusset fabric: 8 in (20 cm) square of print fabric
- Lining fabric: One fat quarter of print fabric
- Foundation fabric: ½ yd (0.5 m) of muslin
- Lightweight fusible fleece: 8 x 17¾ in (20 x 45 cm)
- #25 embroidery floss in pink and light pink
- Pearl cotton #8 in variegated pink
- Small red beads
- 15¾ in (40 cm) of ⅜ in (1 cm) wide lace trim
- One 4¾ x 2⅜ in (12 x 6 cm) sew-in metal clasp

PROJECT DIAGRAM

POUCH OUTSIDES (MAKE 2)

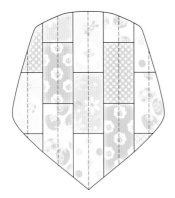

GUSSETS (MAKE 2)

CUTTING INSTRUCTIONS

Trace and cut out the templates on Pattern Sheet B. Use the templates to cut out the following pieces, adding ¼ in (6 mm) seam allowance.

PATCHWORK FABRIC

- 30 patchwork pieces

FUSIBLE FLEECE AND FOUNDATION FABRIC

- 2 pouch outsides

- 2 gussets

GUSSET FABRIC

- 2 gussets

LINING FABRIC

- 2 pouch linings

- 2 gusset linings

Sew using
¼ in (6 mm) seam
allowance, unless
otherwise noted.

CONSTRUCTION STEPS

1. Sew the patchwork pieces together to make two pouch outsides. Adhere fusible fleece to the wrong side of each pouch outside. Layer the foundation fabric underneath and quilt as noted on the template. Embroider and sew the beads on as noted on the template.

Note: This bag is constructed with fusible fleece and a foundation fabric to provide support and structure. A separate lining will be added to hide these layers.

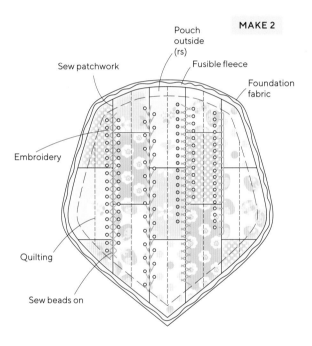

2. Adhere fusible fleece to the wrong side of each gusset. Layer the foundation fabric underneath. Quilt as noted on the template.

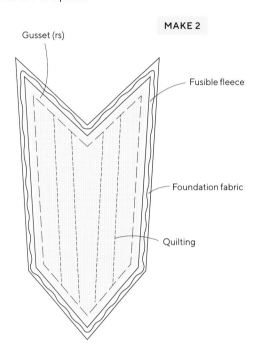

3. Align one pouch outside and one gusset with right sides together. Sew together along one side, stopping at the bottom seam allowance mark.

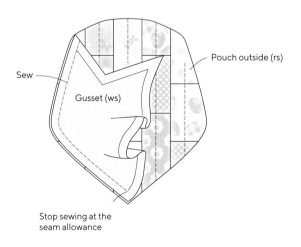

4. Use the same process to attach the remaining pouch outside and gusset.

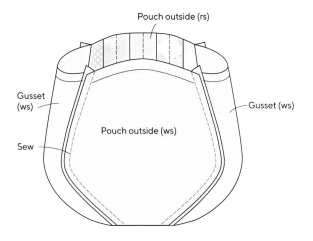

Pouch outside (rs)

Gusset (ws)

Gusset (ws)

Sew

Pouch outside (ws)

5. Use the same process to sew the pouch linings and gusset linings together.

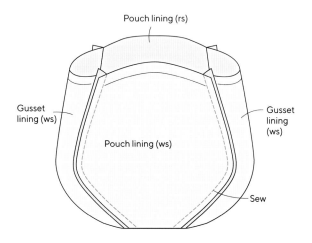

Pouch lining (rs)

Gusset lining (ws)

Gusset lining (ws)

Pouch lining (ws)

Sew

6. Insert the lining into the pouch with right sides together. Sew together around the top, leaving an opening.

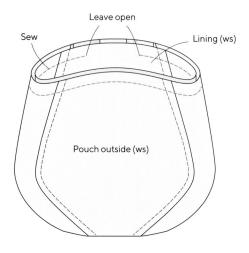

Leave open

Sew

Lining (ws)

Pouch outside (ws)

7. Turn right side out. Fold the opening seam allowance in and hand stitch closed. Tuck the lining into the pouch.

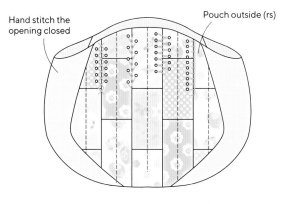

Hand stitch the opening closed

Pouch outside (rs)

8. Insert the pouch into the metal clasp. Baste the pouch to the clasp in several spots to temporarily hold in place.

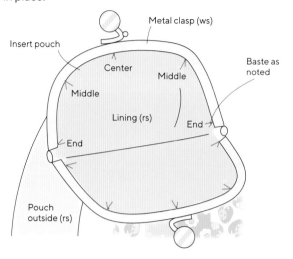

9. Use pearl cotton #8 to backstitch the pouch to the metal clasp. Apply glue to the stitching line on the inside of the pouch. Adhere the lace, then use a flathead screwdriver to tuck the edge of the lace under the metal clasp. The lace will hide the stitching line.

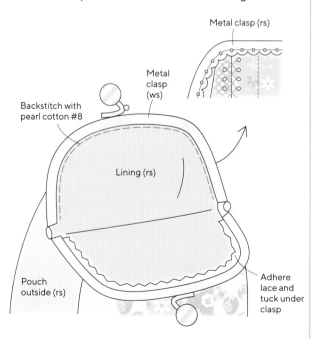

FINISHED DIAGRAM

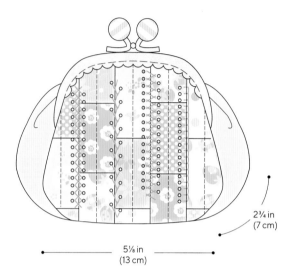

Use your favorite scraps to construct this pretty diamond patchwork skirt.

This adorable dress-shaped pouch features a diamond-shaped patchwork skirt and pretty collar. It's the perfect size for storing a smartphone.

VINTAGE LOVERS PHONE CASE

MATERIALS

- Patchwork fabric: 10 assorted print scraps
- Main fabric: One fat quarter of pink and white polka dot fabric
- Accent fabric: 6 x 3⅛ in (15 x 8 cm) of white floral print fabric
- Lining fabric: One fat eighth of print fabric
- Foundation fabric: ¼ yd (0.3 m) of muslin
- Batting: 15¾ x 8 in (40 x 20 cm)
- Two D-rings with an inner width of ⅜ in (1 cm)
- Two 1½ in (3.5 cm) long swivel hooks
- One ½ in (1.2 cm) diameter button

PROJECT DIAGRAM

FRONT (MAKE 1)

BACK (MAKE 1)

TABS (MAKE 2)

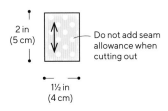

2 in
(5 cm)

Do not add seam
allowance when
cutting out

1½ in
(4 cm)

HANDLE (MAKE 1)

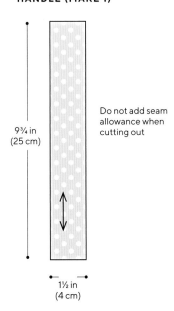

9¾ in
(25 cm)

Do not add seam
allowance when
cutting out

1½ in
(4 cm)

CUTTING INSTRUCTIONS

Trace and cut out the templates on Pattern Sheet D. Use the templates to cut out the following pieces, adding ¼ in (6 mm) seam allowance.

PATCHWORK FABRIC
- 10 patchwork pieces

MAIN FABRIC
- 14 patchwork pieces
- 1 back
- 1 dress top

ACCENT FABRIC
- 1 waistband
- 1 collar

BATTING, FOUNDATION FABRIC, AND LINING
- 1 front
- 1 back

Cut out the following pieces, which do not have templates, according to the dimensions listed below (these include seam allowance):

MAIN FABRIC
- Tabs (cut 2): 2 x 1½ in (5 x 4 cm)
- Handle: 1½ x 9¾ in (4 x 25 cm)

Sew using ¼ in (6 mm) seam allowance, unless otherwise noted.

CONSTRUCTION STEPS

1. Sew the patchwork pieces together to make the front. Appliqué the collar to the front following the placement noted on the template. Layer the front, batting, and foundation fabric. Quilt as noted on the template.

Note: This bag is constructed with fusible fleece and a foundation fabric to provide support and structure. A separate lining will be added to hide these layers.

2. Align the quilted front and front lining with right sides together. Sew together leaving a 2 in (5 cm) opening. Make clips into the seam allowance along the inner curves.

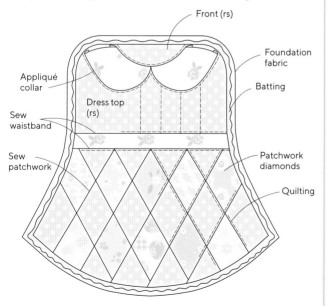

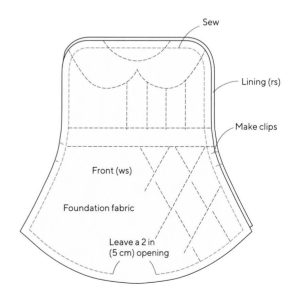

3. Turn right side out. Fold the opening seam allowances in and hand stitch closed. Blind hem stitch around the top to secure the lining in place (only along the bag opening).

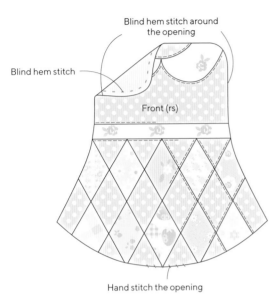

Blind hem stitch around the opening

Blind hem stitch

Front (rs)

Hand stitch the opening

4. Make the tabs: Fold and press the long edges of each tab ⅜ in (1 cm) to the wrong side. Fold in half and topstitch close to each long edge. Thread a D-ring onto each tab, then fold in half.

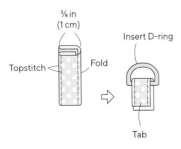

⅜ in (1 cm)

Insert D-ring

Topstitch   Fold

Tab

5. Layer the back, batting, and foundation fabric. Quilt as shown below. Align the quilted back and back lining with right sides together with the tabs sandwiched in between. Sew together, leaving a 2 in (5 cm) opening. Make clips into the seam allowance along the inner curves.

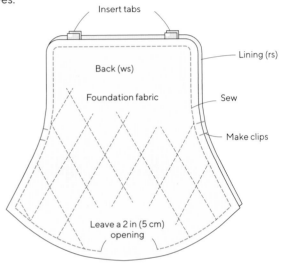

Insert tabs

Lining (rs)

Back (ws)

Foundation fabric

Sew

Make clips

Leave a 2 in (5 cm) opening

6. Turn right side out. Fold the opening seam allowances in and hand stitch closed.

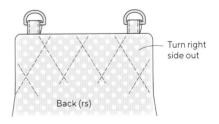

Turn right side out

Back (rs)

7. Align the front and back with right sides together. Whipstitch together along the sides and bottom, stitching through the top layer of fabric only (do not stitch through the lining).

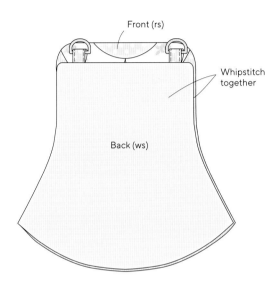

Front (rs)

Whipstitch together

Back (ws)

8. Make the handle: Fold and press the long edges of the handle ⅜ in (1 cm) to the wrong side. Fold in half and topstitch close to each long edge. Thread a swivel hook onto each short end of the handle. Fold each short end over ¼ in (5 mm), then another ⅜ in (1 cm) and topstitch to secure the swivel hook in place.

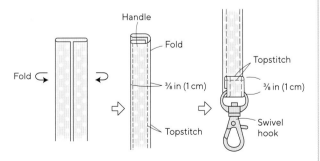

Fold

Handle

Fold

⅜ in (1 cm)

Topstitch

⅜ in (1 cm)

Topstitch

Swivel hook

9. Attach the swivel hooks to the D-rings to complete the handle. Sew a button to the center of the collar following the placement noted on the template.

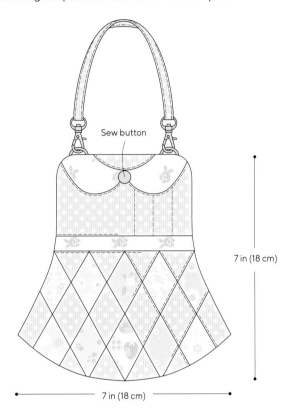

Sew button

7 in (18 cm)

7 in (18 cm)

Have fun mixing and matching print fabrics, then embellishing with decorative rickrack and buttons to suit your personal style.

THE BEST-DRESSED BAG

MATERIALS

- Patchwork fabric: Two print scraps
- Bodice fabric: 13¾ in (35 cm) square of print fabric
- Collar fabric: 11¾ x 4 in (30 x 10 cm) of print fabric
- Skirt fabric: ⅓ yd (0.3 m) of print fabric
- Handle fabric: 2⅜ x 12¾ in (6 x 32 cm) of print fabric
- Lining fabric: ½ yd (0.5 m) of print fabric
- Foundation fabric: ½ yd (0.5 m) of muslin
- Batting: 29½ x 13¾ in (75 x 35 cm)
- 15¾ in (40 cm) of ¼–⅜ in (8–10 mm) wide rickrack
- 25¼ in (64 cm) of ¾ in (2 cm) wide linen tape
- Three ½ in (1.2 cm) diameter buttons

PROJECT DIAGRAM

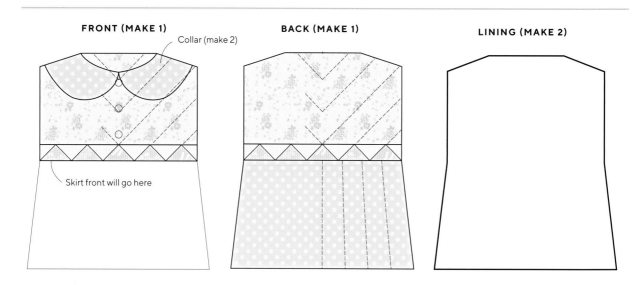

FRONT (MAKE 1)

Collar (make 2)

Skirt front will go here

BACK (MAKE 1)

LINING (MAKE 2)

SKIRT FRONT (MAKE 1)

☆ = Area to gather

¾ in
(2 cm) tuck

HANDLE (MAKE 2)

Do not add seam allowance when cutting out

12¾ in
(32 cm)

1¼ in
(3 cm)

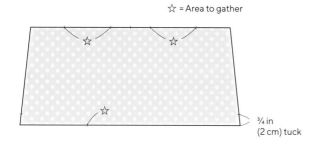
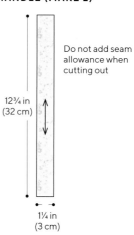

CUTTING INSTRUCTIONS

Trace and cut out the templates on Pattern Sheet B. Use the templates to cut out the following pieces, adding ¼ in (6 mm) seam allowance.

SKIRT FABRIC
- Skirt front/skirt back (cut 1 of each)

PATCHWORK FABRIC
- 22 patchwork triangles (cut 10 of one fabric and 12 of the other)

BODICE FABRIC
- Bodice front/back (cut 1 of each)

BATTING, FOUNDATION FABRIC, AND LINING FABRIC
- 2 dresses

COLLAR FABRIC
- 4 collar pieces (cut 2 symmetrical sets)

Sew using ¼ in (6 mm) seam allowance, unless otherwise noted.

Cut out the following pieces, which do not have templates, according to the dimensions listed below (these include seam allowance):

HANDLE FABRIC
- Handles (cut 2): 1¼ x 12¾ in (3 x 32 cm)

CONSTRUCTION STEPS

1. Sew running stitch in the top and bottom seam allowances of the skirt front (refer to the template for placement). Pull the thread tails to gather the skirt as shown below.

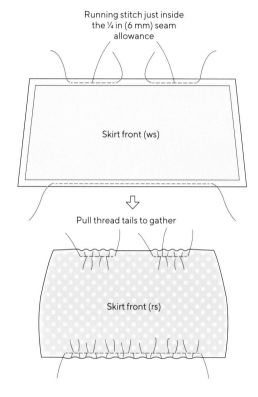

Running stitch just inside the ¼ in (6 mm) seam allowance

Skirt front (ws)

Pull thread tails to gather

Skirt front (rs)

2. Sew 11 patchwork triangles together to make the waistband. Sew the waistband to the skirt front, taking care to align the triangles as shown below. You may need to adjust the gathers to make the skirt fit the waistband. Next, sew the bodice front to the waistband to complete the front.

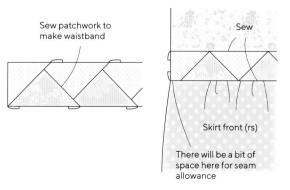

Sew patchwork to make waistband

Sew

Skirt front (rs)

There will be a bit of space here for seam allowance

3. Layer the front, batting, and foundation fabric. Sew all three layers together around the perimeter. Quilt as noted on the template. Mark the collar placement.

Note: This bag is constructed with fusible fleece and a foundation fabric to provide support and structure. A separate lining will be added to hide these layers.

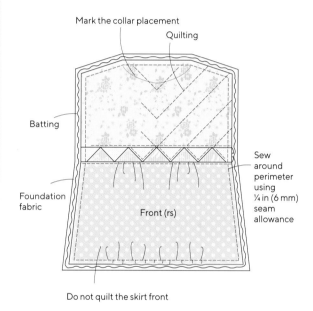

Mark the collar placement

Quilting

Batting

Foundation fabric

Sew around perimeter using ¼ in (6 mm) seam allowance

Front (rs)

Do not quilt the skirt front

4. Repeat steps 2 and 3 to make the back. Note that the skirt back is quilted (refer to the template for quilting lines). There's no need to mark the collar placement on the back.

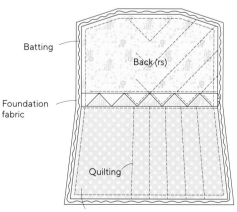

Batting

Back (rs)

Foundation fabric

Quilting

There are no gathers on the skirt back

5. Align the front and back with right sides together. Sew together along the bottom.

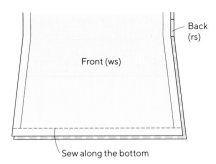

6. Tuck the bottom seam in ¾ in (2 cm) and pin in place. Sew the front and back together along the sides, securing the tuck. Repeat steps 5 and 6 to make the lining, but leave a small opening in one side when sewing the lining pieces together.

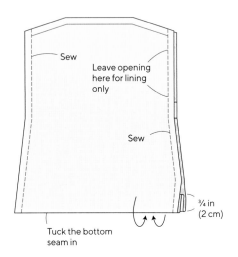

7. Sew or glue the rickrack to two of the collar pieces (refer to the template for placement). Align each rickrack collar piece with a plain collar piece and sew together, leaving the straight edge open. Make clips into the seam allowance along the inner curves. Turn right side out.

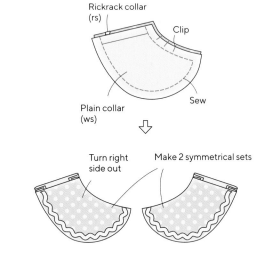

8. Make the handles: Fold and press the long edges of each handle in ⅜ in (1 cm) to the wrong side. Align each handle on top of a 12¾ in (32 cm) long piece of linen tape and topstitch, stitching close to the long edges.

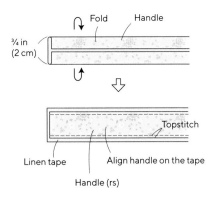

9. Sew the two collar pieces from step 7 to the bag front by machine stitching along the straight edges and hand stitching along the inner curves. Take care to stitch through the bag front only. Finally, sew the handles to the front and back (refer to the template for placement).

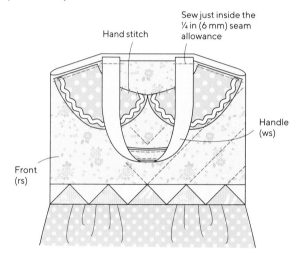

Hand stitch

Sew just inside the ¼ in (6 mm) seam allowance

Handle (ws)

Front (rs)

10. Insert the lining from step 6 into the bag with right sides together. Sew together around the top.

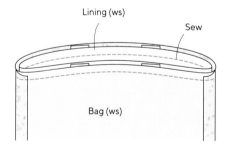

Lining (ws)

Sew

Bag (ws)

11. Turn right side out. Fold the opening seam allowances in and hand stitch closed. Tuck the lining into the bag. Blind hem stitch around the top to secure the lining in place. Sew the buttons to the front following the placement noted on the template.

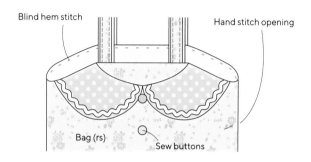

Blind hem stitch

Hand stitch opening

Bag (rs)

Sew buttons

FINISHED DIAGRAM

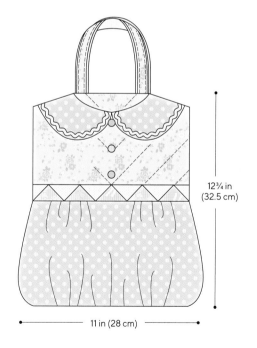

12¾ in (32.5 cm)

11 in (28 cm)

This cute little pouch is the perfect size for storing pens and pencils.

Crazy quilts are made by connecting randomly shaped patchwork pieces to create a dynamic, asymmetric panel. For this design, I kept the fabrics all within the same color family for a cohesive look.

CRAZY QUILT PENCIL CASE

MATERIALS

- Patchwork fabric: Assorted print scraps
- Bottom fabric: 9¾ x 3⅛ in (25 x 8 cm) of print fabric
- Lining fabric: 8 x 9¾ in (20 x 25 cm) of print fabric
- Binding fabric: One 1½ x 29½ in (3.5 x 75 cm) bias strip
- Fusible fleece: 8 x 9¾ in (20 x 25 cm)
- 19¾ in (50 cm) of ⅜ in (1 cm) wide rickrack
- One 8 in (20 cm) zipper

PROJECT DIAGRAM

POUCH (MAKE 1)

Zipper opening

Front

Stitch in the ditch

Rickrack

Bottom

Back

CUTTING INSTRUCTIONS

Trace and cut out the templates on Pattern Sheet C. Use the templates to cut out the following pieces, adding ¼ in (6 mm) seam allowance.

PATCHWORK FABRIC

- Patchwork pieces 1–7 (cut 2 of each)

BOTTOM FABRIC

- 1 bottom (cut on the fold)

FUSIBLE FLEECE AND LINING FABRIC

- 1 pouch

Sew using ¼ in (6 mm) seam allowance, unless otherwise noted.

Cut out the following piece, which does not have a template, according to the dimensions listed below (these include seam allowance):

BINDING FABRIC

- Bias strip: 1½ x 29½ in (3.5 x 75 cm)

CONSTRUCTION STEPS

1. Sew patchwork pieces 1–7 together following the numerical order noted on the template to make a front and back. Sew the long edges of the bottom to the front and back to complete the pouch top. Adhere fusible fleece to the wrong side of the pouch top. Layer the lining underneath and quilt as noted on the template. Hand stitch the rickrack in place, covering the bottom seams (refer to the template for placement).

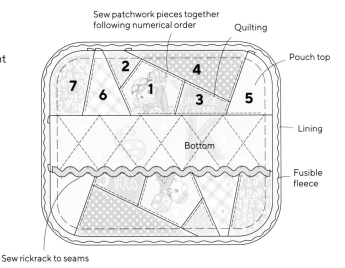

Sew patchwork pieces together following numerical order

Quilting

Pouch top

Lining

Fusible fleece

Sew rickrack to seams

Bottom

2. With right sides together, align the binding with the perimeter of the pouch top. Fold the short ends as noted in the diagram below and overlap. Sew the binding in place, wrap it around the raw edges, and hand stitch to the lining.

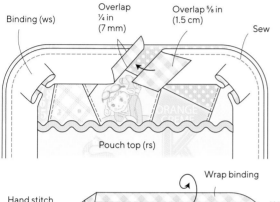

3. Fold the pouch in half with right sides together. Whipstitch the sides together, stopping at the mark noted on the template. To miter the corners, align each side seam with the bottom fold and sew across the corner with a 1 in (2.5 cm) long seam.

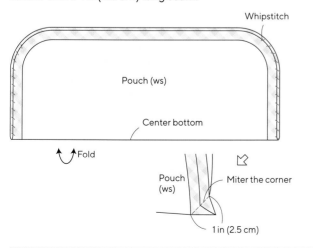

4. Align the right side of the opened zipper with the bindings on the inside of the pouch (refer to the template for placement). Blind hem stitch the zipper to the binding. Catch stitch the long raw edges of the zipper to the lining and hem stitch the short raw edges in place.

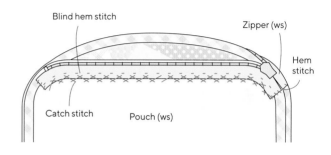

FINISHED DIAGRAM

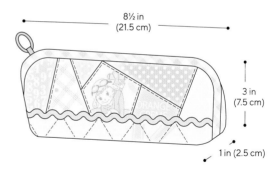

When designing this pouch, I started by selecting a fun novelty fabric for the center, then added coordinating prints for the surrounding pieces. Look for a zipper with a decorative charm for an extra special touch.

CRAZY QUILT ZIP POUCH

MATERIALS

- Patchwork fabric: Seven assorted print scraps
- Bottom fabric: 9¾ x 3⅛ in (25 x 8 cm) of print fabric
- Lining fabric: One fat quarter of print fabric
- Binding fabric: Two 1½ x 9¾ in (3.5 x 25 cm) bias strips
- Fusible fleece: 11¾ x 13¾ in (30 x 35 cm)
- 24 in (60 cm) of ⅜ in (1 cm) wide lace
- One 8 in (20 cm) zipper

PROJECT DIAGRAM

POUCH (MAKE 1)

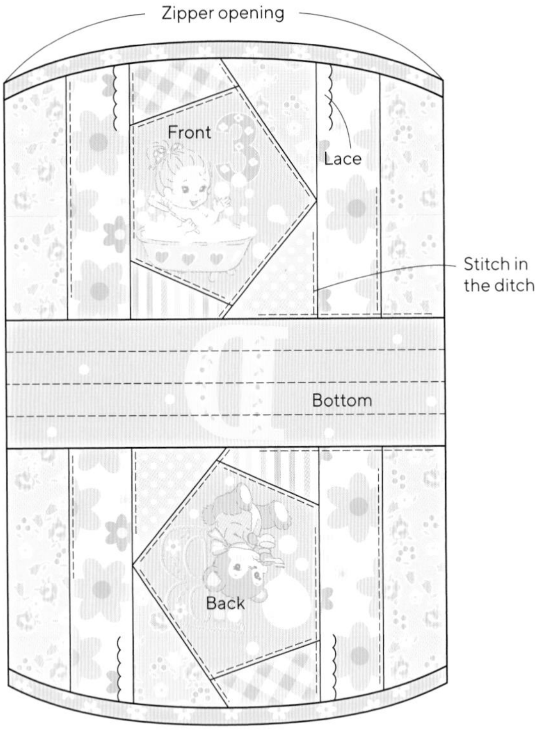

CUTTING INSTRUCTIONS

Trace and cut out the templates on Pattern Sheet C. Use the templates to cut out the following pieces, adding ¼ in (6 mm) seam allowance.

PATCHWORK FABRIC

- Patchwork pieces 1-5 (cut 2 of each)
- Patchwork pieces 6 and 7 (cut 4 of each)

BOTTOM FABRIC

- 1 bottom (cut on the fold)

FUSIBLE FLEECE AND LINING FABRIC

- 1 pouch

Cut out the following pieces, which do not have templates, according to the dimensions listed below (these include seam allowance):

BINDING FABRIC

- Bias strips (cut 2): 1½ x 9¾ in (3.5 x 25 cm)

LINING FABRIC

- Bias strips for side seams (cut 2):
  1½ x 5½ in (3.5 x 14 cm)

Sew using
¼ in (6 mm) seam
allowance, unless
otherwise noted.

CONSTRUCTION STEPS

1. Sew patchwork pieces 1-7 together following the numerical order noted on the template to make a front and back. Sew the long edges of the bottom to the front and back to complete the pouch top. Adhere fusible fleece to the wrong side of the pouch top. Layer the lining underneath and quilt as noted on the template. Hand stitch the lace to the front following the placement noted on the template. Bind the top and bottom edges of the pouch.

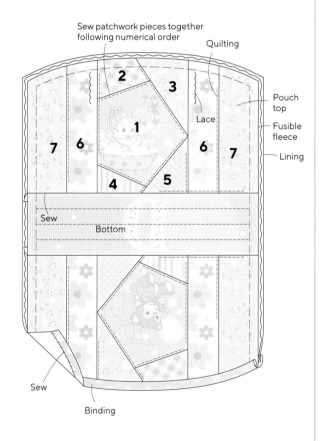

2. Fold the pouch in half with right sides together. Sew together along the sides. Bind the seam allowances. To miter the corners, align each side seam with the bottom fold and sew across the corner with a 2⅜ in (6 cm) long seam.

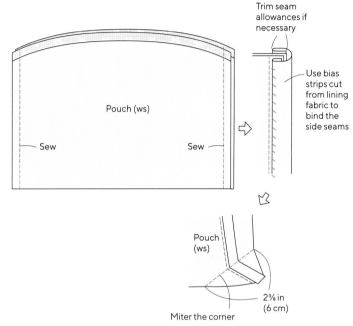

3. Install the zipper as shown in step 4 on page 83.

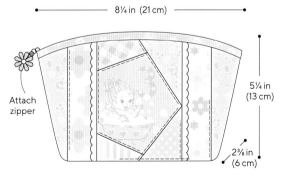

QUILTED HOME

This collection of colorful quilts and accessories will brighten up any room. I have always been inspired by the vibrant colors and unique shapes of fruit and flowers, so I've designed these projects in celebration of my favorite motifs.

The wreath also works
well as a centerpiece
for your table.

Welcome the arrival of spring with this cheerful wreath featuring three-dimensional patchwork strawberries, delicate white flowers, and embroidered green leaves.

STRAWBERRY BLOSSOM WREATH

MATERIALS

- White flower fabric: ½ yd (0.5 m) of solid white fabric
- Pink flower fabric: One fat quarter of pink floral print fabric
- Calyx fabric: One fat eighth of solid green fabric
- Strawberry fabric: Four assorted red and pink print scraps
- Leaf and hull fabric: Assorted green scraps
- Leaf backing fabric: Solid green fabric
- Fusible web
- Cotton stuffing
- ⅛ in (3 mm) thick green waxed cord
- 22-gauge green floral wire
- ⅜ in (1 cm) diameter white flower-shaped lace appliqués (about 20)
- Green floral tape
- #25 embroidery floss in green
- One 12 in (30 cm) diameter wreath form

CUTTING INSTRUCTIONS

Trace and cut out the templates on Pattern Sheet D. Use the templates to cut out the following pieces, adding ¼ in (6 mm) seam allowance.

WHITE FLOWER FABRIC
- 75 petals

PINK FLOWER FABRIC
- 25 petals

STRAWBERRY FABRIC
- 9 small strawberry pieces
- 51 medium strawberry pieces
- 18 large strawberry pieces

Use the templates to cut out the following pieces, but do not add seam allowance.

CALYX FABRIC
- 20 calyxes

LEAF AND HULL FABRIC
- 3 small hulls
- 17 medium hulls
- 6 large hulls

Sew using ¼ in (6 mm) seam allowance, unless otherwise noted.

CONSTRUCTION STEPS

1. Make the petals: Align two petals pieces with right sides together. Sew together around the curve, leaving the bottom open. Turn right side out. Repeat process to make a total of five petals. Align the petals in a row so they overlap ¼ in (5 mm) at the bottom. Using two strands of thread, sew the petals together using running stitch. Insert the needle back into the first petal and sew another row of running stitch on that petal only.

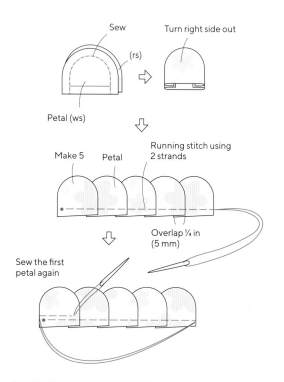

Sew

(rs)

Turn right side out

Petal (ws)

Make 5 Petal Running stitch using 2 strands

Overlap ¼ in (5 mm)

Sew the first petal again

2. Make a flower: Pull the thread tails taut to form the petals into a flower shape, then knot to secure. Fold and press the raw edge of a calyx piece over ⅛ in (3 mm) to the wrong side. Punch a hole in the center using a stiletto. Hand stitch the calyx to the wrong side of the flower. Fold a small piece of wire in half and insert through a flower-shaped lace appliqué. Next, insert the wire through the center of the flower.

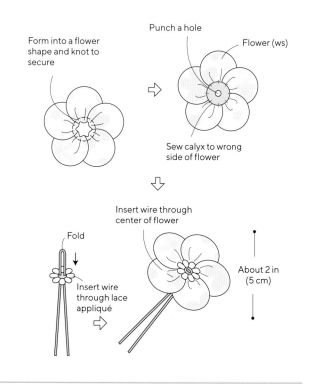

Form into a flower shape and knot to secure

Punch a hole

Flower (ws)

Sew calyx to wrong side of flower

Insert wire through center of flower

Fold

Insert wire through lace appliqué

About 2 in (5 cm)

3. Repeat steps 1 and 2 to make a total of 20 flowers (refer to chart below for quantities of each color).

COLOR	QUANTITY
White	15
Pink	5

4. Make a strawberry: Align two strawberry pieces with right sides together. Sew together along one curved side, stopping at the bottom seam allowance mark. Next, align the third strawberry piece with right sides together and sew along the two remaining curves using the same process. Turn right side out.

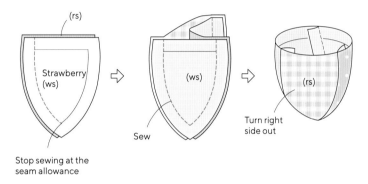

5. Sew the hull to the strawberry: Fold the hull in half with right sides together. Sew together along the short straight edge. Press the seam allowance open and turn right side out. Position the hull on the right side of the strawberry, aligning the top edges.

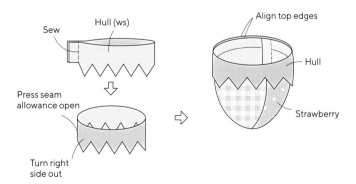

6. Fold the top seam allowance of both the hull and strawberry over ¼ in (5 mm) to the wrong side. Sew running stitch around the top edge, leaving long thread tails. Insert stuffing. Next, knot a 4-6 in (10-15 cm) long piece of cord and insert the knotted end into the strawberry. Pull the thread tails to gather the strawberry closed and secure with a knot. Stitch through the cord 2-3 times, then bring the needle out on the other side and knot again. Wrap a piece of wire around the end of the cord, then secure with floral tape.

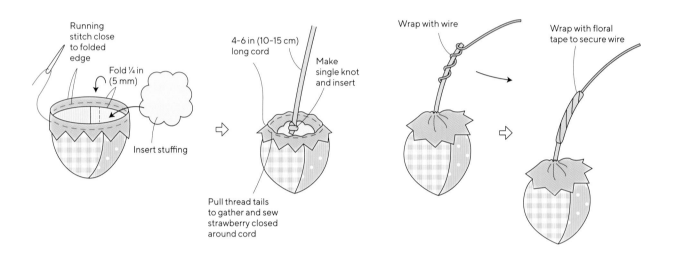

7. Repeat steps 4-6 to make 26 total strawberries in the sizes noted below.

	QUANTITY	SIZE
SMALL	3	1¼ in (3 cm)
MEDIUM	17	1⅜ in (3.5 cm)
LARGE	6	1½ in (4 cm)

8. Use the template to mark the cutting lines and embroidery design for 25 leaves on the right side of the leaf fabrics. Embroider, then trim into shape along the indented bottom curve only. Use fusible web to adhere the leaf fabrics to backing fabric with 3-3½ in (8-9 cm) long wires sandwiched between the layers of fabric for the leaf stems. Finally, trim each leaf into shape and iron again to secure. Make 25 leaves total.

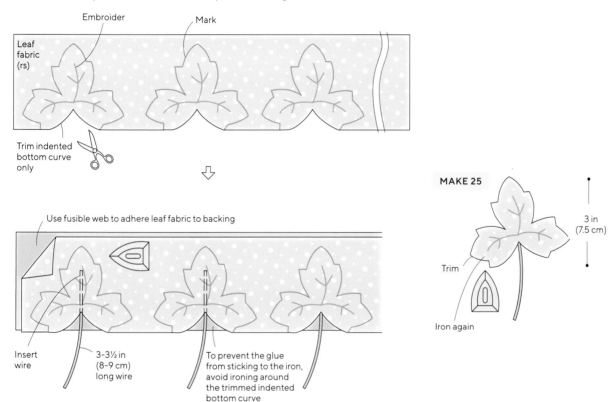

9. Use the wires to attach the strawberries, flowers, and leaves to the wreath form as desired. Try to achieve balance among the three components.

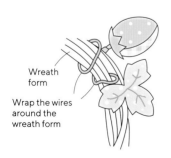

FINISHED DIAGRAM

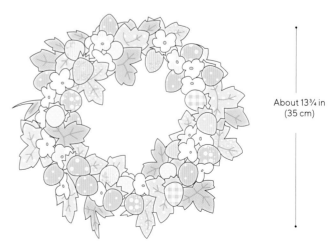

About 13¾ in (35 cm)

These sweet little accessories use the same fruit and flower patterns as the Strawberry Blossom Wreath to create a cheerful brooch. Pin a corsage to your favorite sweater or bag to brighten up any outfit.

STRAWBERRY CORSAGES

MATERIALS

- Flower fabric: 9¾ x 4 in (25 x 10 cm) of solid white fabric
- Strawberry fabric: Assorted print scraps, about 7 x 3⅛ in (18 x 8 cm) each
- Calyx, leaf, and hull fabric: Assorted green scraps
- Cotton stuffing
- 8-12 in (20-30 cm) of ⅛ in (3 mm) thick green waxed cord
- 8-12 in (20-30 cm) of 22-gauge green floral wire
- One ⅜ in (1 cm) diameter white flower-shaped lace appliqué
- 12 in (30 cm) of ⅜ in (1 cm) wide white lace
- One 1 in (2.5 cm) brooch pin
- #25 embroidery floss in green and yellow

CUTTING INSTRUCTIONS

Trace and cut out the templates on Pattern Sheet D. Use the templates to cut out the following pieces, adding ¼ in (6 mm) seam allowance.

FLOWER FABRIC
• 5 petals

CALYX, LEAF, AND HULL FABRIC
• 4 leaf pieces

STRAWBERRY FABRIC
• 3 strawberry pieces for each strawberry (select desired size and number of strawberries)

Use the templates to cut out the following pieces, but do not add seam allowance.

CALYX, LEAF, AND HULL FABRIC
• 1 calyx
• 1 hull for each strawberry (use correct size)

CONSTRUCTION STEPS

1. Make the petals as shown in step 1 on page 92.

2. Make a flower: Pull the thread tails taut to form the petals into a flower shape, then knot to secure. Fold and press the raw edge of a calyx piece over ⅛ in (3 mm) to the wrong side. Hand stitch the calyx to the wrong side of the flower. Use two strands of yellow thread to sew a flower-shaped lace appliqué to center of the flower on the right side.

3. Make the leaves: To make each leaf, align two leaf pieces with right sides together. Sew leaving a small opening, as noted on the template. Turn right side out, fold the opening seam allowances in, and hand stitch closed. Embroider as noted on the template. Make two leaves total.

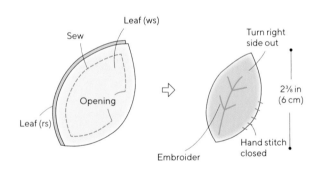

Sew

Leaf (ws)

Leaf (rs)

Opening

Turn right side out

Embroider

Hand stitch closed

2⅜ in (6 cm)

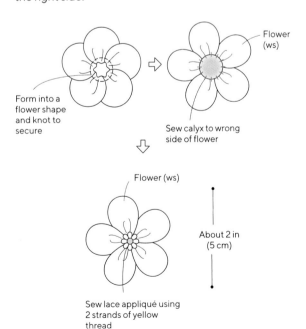

Form into a flower shape and knot to secure

Sew calyx to wrong side of flower

Flower (ws)

Flower (ws)

About 2 in (5 cm)

Sew lace appliqué using 2 strands of yellow thread

Sew using ¼ in (6 mm) seam allowance, unless otherwise noted.

4. Make two or three strawberries, as shown in steps 4–6 on pages 93–94, but for the corsage, insert a piece of wire into a 4–6 in (10–15 cm) long piece of cord before attaching to the strawberry. Then apply a dab of glue to the end of each cord.

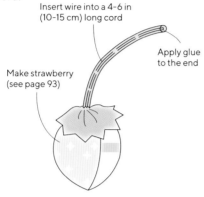

Insert wire into a 4–6 in (10–15 cm) long cord

Apply glue to the end

Make strawberry (see page 93)

5. Assemble the corsage: Tie the lace into a bow. Hand stitch the bow and the strawberry cords to the calyx on the wrong side of the flower.

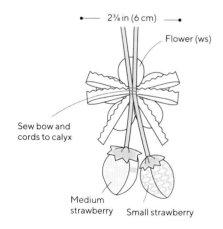

2⅜ in (6 cm)

Flower (ws)

Sew bow and cords to calyx

Medium strawberry

Small strawberry

6. Hand stitch the leaves to the wrong side of the flower, then hand stitch a brooch pin to the calyx.

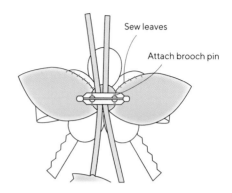

Sew leaves

Attach brooch pin

FINISHED DIAGRAM

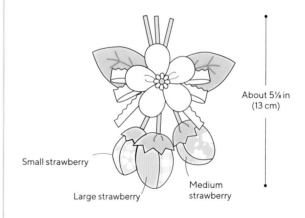

About 5⅛ in (13 cm)

Small strawberry

Large strawberry

Medium strawberry

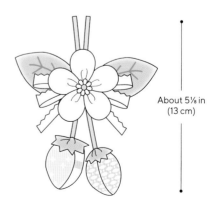

About 5⅛ in (13 cm)

No matter the time of the year, you'll feel like spring is in the air with these fruit-themed mini quilts. These two variations feature the same motif, but have a completely different effect based on the technique used—embroidery or appliqué—the choice is yours!

FRESH & SWEET FRAMED MINI QUILTS

MATERIALS

FOR THE EMBROIDERED VARIATION

- Background fabric: 10 in (25 cm) square of solid white fabric
- Patchwork fabric: Six assorted print scraps
- Batting: 12 in (30 cm) square
- Backing fabric: 12 in (30 cm) square of muslin fabric
- #25 embroidery floss in pink, light pink, brown, green, dark green, yellow, and red
- Frame with an inner size of 9½ in (24 cm) square

FOR THE APPLIQUÉ VARIATION

- Background fabric: 10 in (25 cm) square of solid white fabric
- Patchwork fabric: Six assorted print scraps
- Appliqué fabric: Assorted print scraps
- Batting: 12 in (30 cm) square
- Backing fabric: 12 in (30 cm) square of muslin fabric
- Four ¾ in (2.1 cm) diameter white flower-shaped lace appliqués
- #25 embroidery floss in brown, green, dark green, and yellow
- Frame with an inner size of 9½ in (24 cm) square

CUTTING INSTRUCTIONS

Trace and cut out the templates on Pattern Sheet D. Use the templates to cut out the following pieces, adding ⅛ in (3 mm) seam allowance.

**APPLIQUÉ FABRIC
(FOR THE APPLIQUÉ VARIATION ONLY)**

- Fruit motifs

Use the templates to cut out the following pieces, adding ¼ in (6 mm) seam allowance.

PATCHWORK FABRIC

- 30 A pieces

Sew using ¼ in (6 mm) seam allowance, unless otherwise noted.

CONSTRUCTION STEPS

1. Embroider and/or appliqué the motif to the background fabric.

2. Sew the A pieces together into two sets of six and two sets of eight. Sew the sets of six to the left and right edges of the background fabric, then sew the sets of eight to the top and bottom.

3. Layer the assembled top, batting, and backing. Quilt as noted on the template. For the embroidered variation, do not quilt over the embroidery—instead, bring the quilting thread under the embroidery stitches.

4. For the appliquéd variation only, straight stitch the lace appliqués in place using two strands of yellow thread (refer to the template for placement).

5. Trim the raw edges of the mini quilt with pinking shears to prevent fraying.

6. Mount the mini quilt in a frame.

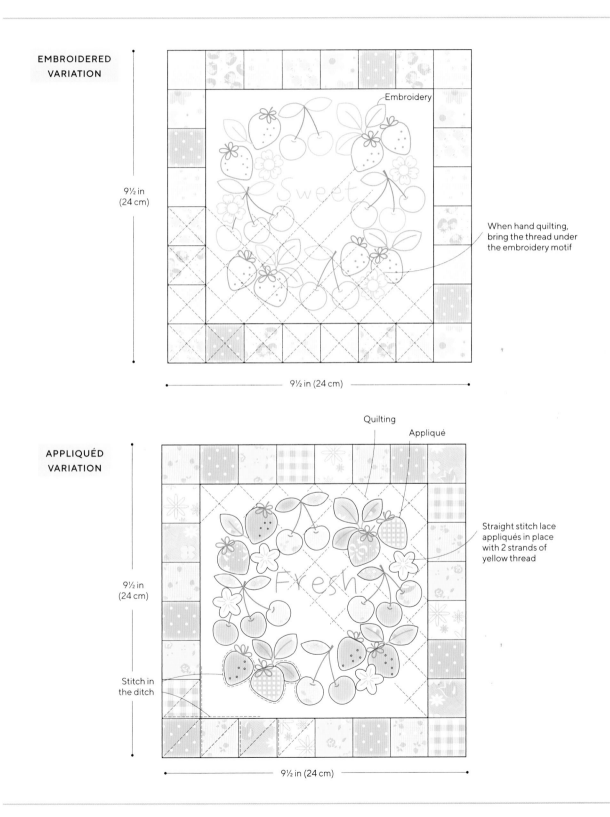

EMBROIDERED
VARIATION

Embroidery

When hand quilting,
bring the thread under
the embroidery motif

Sweet

9½ in
(24 cm)

9½ in (24 cm)

Quilting

Appliqué

APPLIQUÉD
VARIATION

Straight stitch lace
appliqués in place
with 2 strands of
yellow thread

Fresh

9½ in
(24 cm)

Stitch in
the ditch

9½ in (24 cm)

Yoyos are the perfect shape for recreating a bunch of juicy grapes out of fabric. Use these fun ornaments to decorate your walls or a cupboard.

YOYO GRAPE ORNAMENTS

MATERIALS

- Grape fabric: Assorted purple and green print scraps
- Leaf fabric: 8¾ x 4¾ in (22 x 12 cm) of green print fabric (for each leaf)
- ⅜ in (1 cm) diameter white flower shaped lace appliqués (3 for small bunch or 5 for large bunch)
- 8 in (20 cm) of 22-gauge green floral wire
- #25 embroidery floss in green and yellow

CUTTING INSTRUCTIONS

Trace and cut out the templates on Pattern Sheet D. Use the templates to cut out the following pieces, but do not add seam allowance.

GRAPE FABRIC
- 9 yoyos for small bunch or 15–17 yoyos for large bunch*

LEAF FABRIC
- 2 small leaves for small bunch or 4 large leaves for large bunch

***Note:** There are two different yoyo sizes, which are labeled A and B on the pattern sheet. Refer to the Finished Diagrams on page 107 for the quantities to make of each yoyo size.

Sew using ¼ in (6 mm) seam allowance, unless otherwise noted.

CONSTRUCTION STEPS

1. Use the templates to make the yoyos as shown below. You'll need nine yoyos for the small bunch and 15–17 yoyos for the large bunch. Note that each bunch is composed of two different size yoyos (A and B).

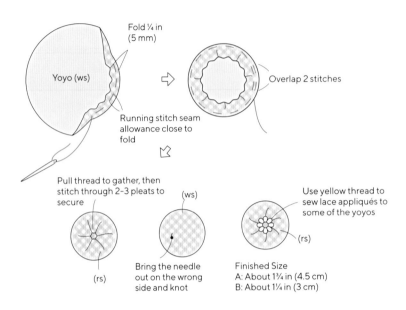

Fold ¼ in (5 mm)

Yoyo (ws)

Running stitch seam allowance close to fold

Overlap 2 stitches

Pull thread to gather, then stitch through 2–3 pleats to secure

(ws)

Use yellow thread to sew lace appliqués to some of the yoyos

(rs)

(rs)

Bring the needle out on the wrong side and knot

Finished Size
A: About 1¾ in (4.5 cm)
B: About 1¼ in (3 cm)

2. Make the leaf or leaves: Embroider each leaf as noted on the template. Align two leaves with right sides together and sew, leaving a small opening. Make clips into the corner seam allowances and turn right side out. Insert a piece of wire into the tip of each leaf. Fold the opening seam allowances in and hand stitch closed.

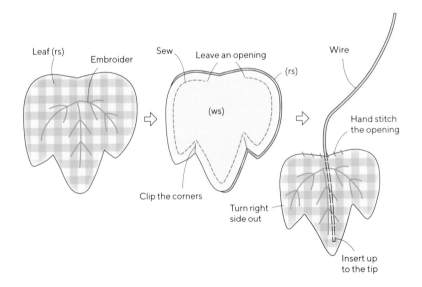

Leaf (rs)

Embroider

Sew

Leave an opening

(rs)

Wire

(ws)

Clip the corners

Turn right side out

Hand stitch the opening

Insert up to the tip

3. Arrange the yoyos into desired shape and hand stitch together on the wrong side (refer to the Finished Diagram below for yoyo A and B placement). Fold a piece of wire a few inches from one end and sew to the wrong side of the bunch of grapes. Wrap the other end of the wire around a stiletto several times to create a curled vine. Use your fingers to adjust the shape of the wire as desired. Finally, sew the wire from the leaf or leaves to the wrong side of the bunch.

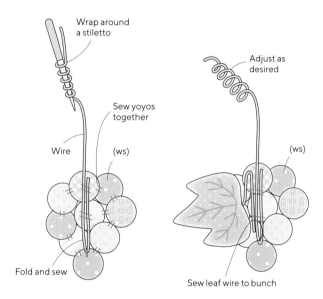

FINISHED DIAGRAM

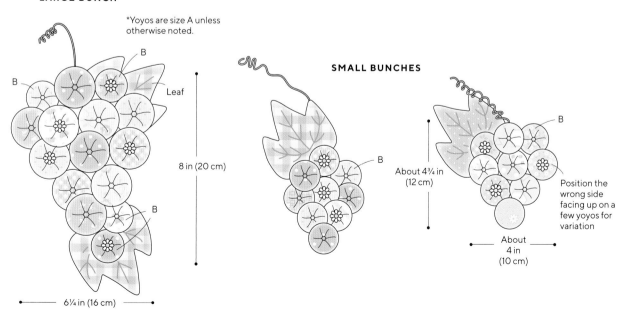

LARGE BUNCH

*Yoyos are size A unless otherwise noted.

B

B

Leaf

8 in (20 cm)

B

6¼ in (16 cm)

SMALL BUNCHES

B

About 4¾ in (12 cm)

B

About 4 in (10 cm)

Position the wrong side facing up on a few yoyos for variation

Decorate a picnic basket with these colorful grape corsages.

With their plump shape and vibrant prints, these grapes have that same juicy look as their real life counterparts. This cheerful accessory makes a great addition to a bag or basket.

GRAPE CORSAGES

MATERIALS

- Grape fabric: Assorted purple and green print scraps
- Two green leaf-shaped lace appliqués
- Cotton stuffing
- 2 in (5 cm) of ⅛ in (3 mm) thick green cord
- 8 in (20 cm) of 22-gauge green floral wire
- 16 in (40 cm) of ½ in (1.2 cm) wide lace
- One 1 in (2.5 cm) brooch pin

CUTTING INSTRUCTIONS

Trace and cut out the templates on Pattern Sheet D. Use the templates to cut out the following pieces, but do not add seam allowance.

GRAPE FABRIC

- 8 grapes
- 8 bottoms

Sew using ¼ in (6 mm) seam allowance, unless otherwise noted.

CONSTRUCTION STEPS

1. Make the grapes: Running stitch around the circumference of each grape and bottom, leaving long thread tails. Insert stuffing into each grape and pull the thread tails to gather the grape closed. Knot to secure. Fold and press the seam allowance in on the wrong side of each bottom, then hand stitch to each grape.

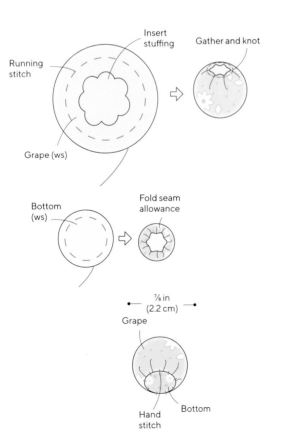

2. Arrange the eight grapes into a bunch as shown below, then hand stitch together on the wrong side.

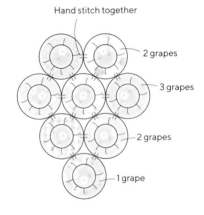

3. Apply a dab of glue to one end of the wire, then insert all the way into the cord. Wrap the extending end of the wire around a stiletto several times to create a curled vine.

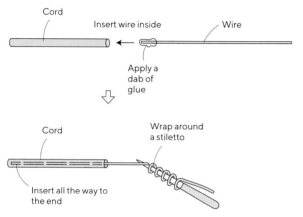

Cord
Insert wire inside
Wire
Apply a dab of glue

Cord
Wrap around a stiletto
Insert all the way to the end

4. Sew the lace appliqués and cord to the wrong side of the bunch. Tie the lace into a bow and sew in place on the wrong side of the bunch.

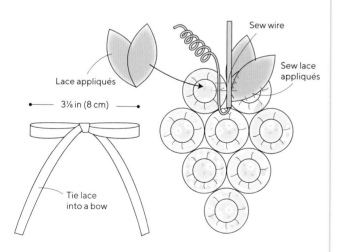

Lace appliqués
Sew wire
Sew lace appliqués
3⅛ in (8 cm)
Tie lace into a bow

5. Sew a brooch pin to the wrong side of the bunch. Bend the end of the cord to create a curved stem.

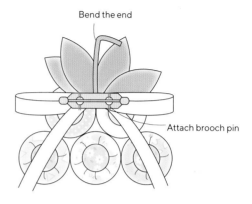

Bend the end
Attach brooch pin

FINISHED DIAGRAM

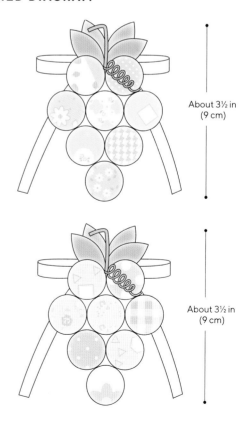

About 3½ in (9 cm)

About 3½ in (9 cm)

With vibrant colors and bold prints, this quilt reminds me of a kaleidoscope of flowers bursting to life. An appliquéd floral border adds another layer of interest to this show-stopping design.

BLOOMING FLOWERS QUILT

MATERIALS

- Patchwork fabric: Assorted print scraps
- Appliqué fabric: Assorted print scraps
- Border fabric: 2¼ yds (1.9 m) of 42 in (106.5 cm) wide fabric
- Backing fabric: 4¼ yds (3.7 m) of 43¼ in (110 cm) wide print fabric
- Batting: 47¼ x 145¾ in (120 x 370 cm)
- Binding fabric: ½ yd (0.5 m) of print fabric

PROJECT DIAGRAM

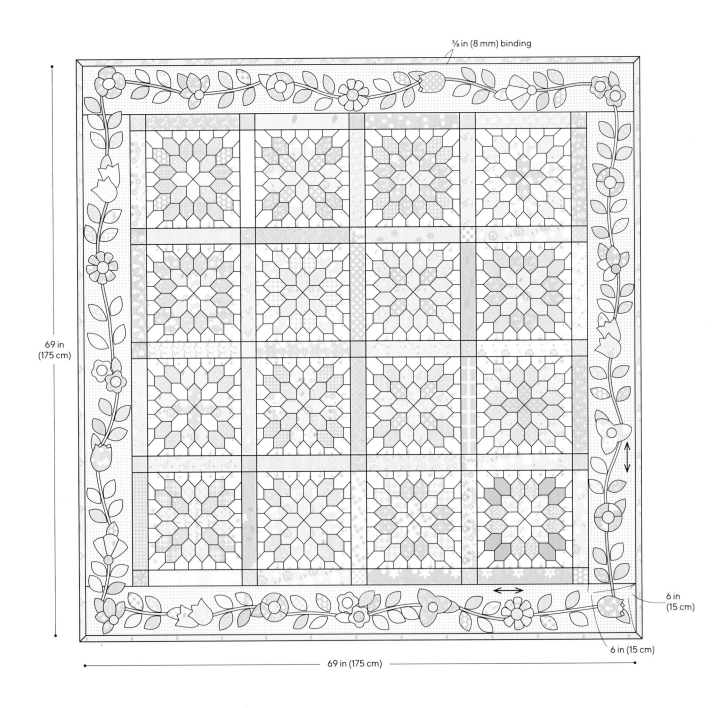

⅜ in (8 mm) binding

69 in
(175 cm)

6 in
(15 cm)

6 in (15 cm)

69 in (175 cm)

Quilting

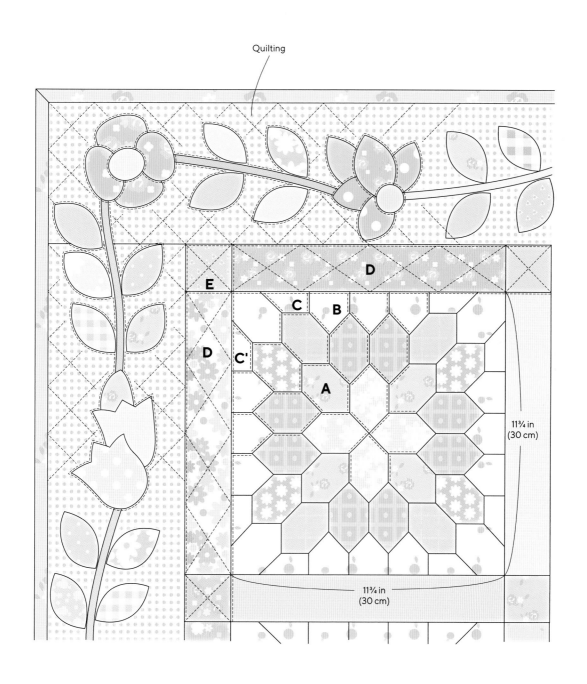

E

D

C B

D C'

A

11¾ in
(30 cm)

11¾ in
(30 cm)

CUTTING INSTRUCTIONS

Trace and cut out the templates on Pattern Sheet C. Use the templates to cut out the following pieces, adding ¼ in (6 mm) seam allowance.

PATCHWORK FABRIC

- 448 A pieces
- 193 B pieces
- 64 C pieces
- 64 C' pieces
- 40 D pieces
- 25 E pieces

Use the templates to cut out the following pieces, adding ⅛ in (3 mm) seam allowance.

APPLIQUÉ FABRIC

- Floral motif

Sew using ¼ in (6 mm) seam allowance, unless otherwise noted.

Cut out the following pieces, which do not have templates, according to the dimensions listed below (these include seam allowance):

BORDER FABRIC

- Side borders (cut 2): See step 5 below, borders will measure abou 6½ x 57½ in (16.2 x 146.2 cm)
- Top and bottom borders (cut 2): See step 6 below, borders will measure abou 6½ x 69½ in (16.2 x 176.2 cm)

BINDING FABRIC

- Binding: 8 yds (7.3 m) of 1½ in (3.5 cm) wide bias strips

CONSTRUCTION STEPS

1. Sew the A–C and C' pieces together to make 16 blocks total. Refer to the diagram on page 115 for layout and the photos on pages 112 and 117 for fabric placement ideas.

2. Alternately sew D pieces and blocks together in rows of four. Make four rows.

3. Make the lattice by alternately sewing five E pieces and four D pieces together. Make five lattice rows.

4. Alternately sew the lattice rows from step 3 with the block rows from step 2.

5. To add the side borders, measure the height of the pieced quilt top at both sides and the middle. Calculate the average height, then add ½ in (1.2 cm) for seam allowance. Trim the side borders to that measurement. Pin and sew the borders to the pieced panel.

6. To add the top and bottom borders, measure the width of the quilt (including the side borders) at the top, middle, and bottom. Calculate the average width, then add ½ in (1.2 cm) for seam allowance. Trim the top and bottom borders to that measurement. Pin and sew the borders to the quilt.

7. Appliqué the floral motif to the borders (refer to the diagram on page 114 for layout).

8. Sew two pieces of batting together in order to achieve a width of 73 in (185 cm). Piece the backing together as necessary.

9. Layer the quilt top, batting, and backing. Quilt as noted in the diagram on page 115.

10. Bind the quilt.

Try your hand at fashion design with this pretty mini quilt. Have fun selecting fabrics for each block, then embellishing with buttons and decorative trims. I chose red and white border fabrics to complement the vintage prints used for the dresses.

DANCING DRESSES QUILT

MATERIALS

- Dress fabric: Nine 6 x 8 in (15 x 20 cm) dark print fabrics
- Dress accent fabric: Nine 4 in (10 cm) square dark print fabrics
- Patchwork background fabric: Nine 9¾ x 8 in (25 x 20 cm) light print fabrics
- Lattice fabric: ½ yd (0.5 m) of red print fabric
- Lattice accent fabric: Assorted print scraps
- Appliqué fabric: Assorted print scraps
- Border fabric: ¾ yd (0.7 m) of white polka dot fabric
- Backing fabric: 1 yd (1 m) of print fabric
- Batting: 31½ x 31½ in (80 x 80 cm)
- Binding fabric: ½ yd (0.5 m) of red gingham fabric
- Nine assorted buttons and charms

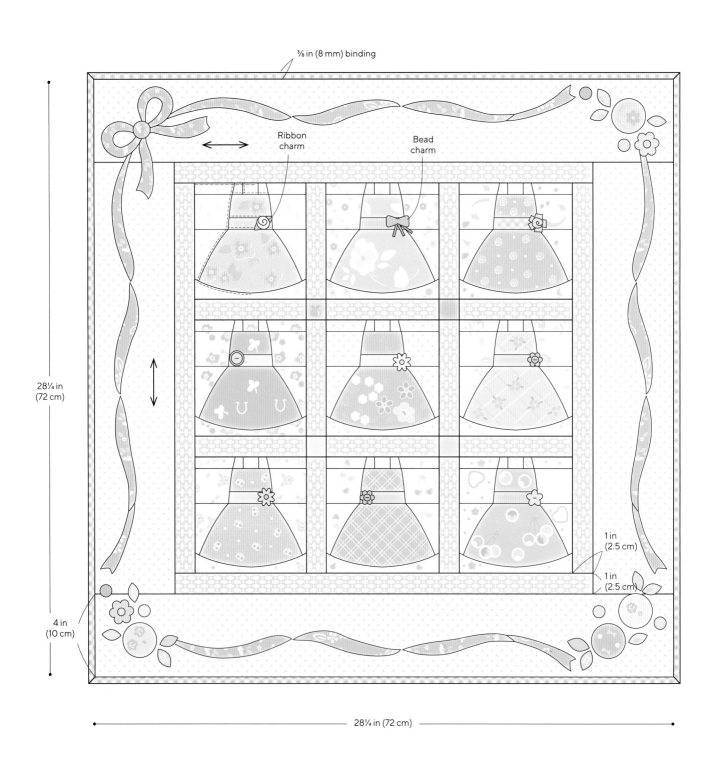

⅜ in (8 mm) binding

Ribbon charm

Bead charm

28¼ in (72 cm)

1 in (2.5 cm)

1 in (2.5 cm)

4 in (10 cm)

28¼ in (72 cm)

CUTTING INSTRUCTIONS

Trace and cut out the templates on Pattern Sheet C. Use the templates to cut out the following pieces, adding ¼ in (6 mm) seam allowance.

DRESS FABRIC
- 9 A pieces
- 9 B pieces

DRESS ACCENT FABRIC
- 9 C pieces
- 9 D pieces
- 9 D' pieces

PATCHWORK BACKGROUND FABRIC
- 9 E pieces
- 9 E' pieces
- 9 F pieces
- 9 G pieces
- 9 G' pieces
- 9 H pieces
- 9 H' pieces
- 9 I pieces

LATTICE FABRIC
- 12 J pieces

LATTICE ACCENT FABRIC
- 4 K pieces

Use the templates to cut out the following pieces, adding ⅛ in (3 mm) seam allowance.

APPLIQUÉ FABRIC
- Ribbon and floral motif

Sew using ¼ in (6 mm) seam allowance, unless otherwise noted.

Cut out the following pieces, which do not have templates, according to the dimensions listed below (these include seam allowance):

LATTICE FABRIC
- Thin borders for left and right edges (cut 2): 1½ x 19 in (3.7 x 48.2 cm)
- Thin borders for top and bottom edges (cut 2): 1½ x 20¾ in (3.7 x 52.3 cm)

BORDER FABRIC
- Thick side borders: 4½ x 21 in (11.2 x 53.2 cm)
- Thick top and bottom borders: 4½ x 28¾ in (11.2 x 73.2 cm)

BINDING FABRIC
- Binding: 3½ yds (3.1 m) of 1½ in (3.5 cm) wide bias strips

CONSTRUCTION STEPS

1. Sew pieces A–I together to make 9 blocks total. Refer to the diagram on page 122 for layout.

2. Alternately sew blocks and J pieces together in rows of three. Make three rows.

3. Make the lattice by alternately sewing three J pieces and two K pieces together. Make two lattice rows.

4. Alternately sew the block rows from step 2 with the lattice rows from step 3. Next, sew the thin borders to the left and right edges of the pieced panel, and then sew the thin borders to the top and bottom edges.

5. Sew the thick side borders to the left and right edges of the quilt.

6. Sew the thick borders to the top and bottom edges of the quilt.

7. Appliqué the ribbon and floral motif to the borders (refer to the pattern sheet for placement).

8. Layer the quilt top, batting, and backing. Quilt as noted in the diagram on page 122.

9. Bind the quilt.

10. Sew the buttons and charms in place.

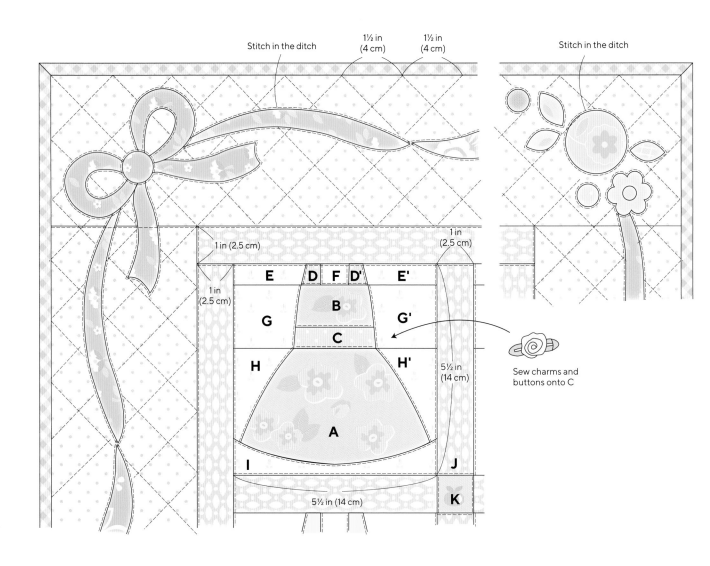

Stitch in the ditch

1½ in (4 cm)

1½ in (4 cm)

Stitch in the ditch

1 in (2.5 cm)

1 in (2.5 cm)

1 in (2.5 cm)

E   D F D'   E'

B

G   G'

C

H   H'

5½ in (14 cm)

A

I   J

K

5½ in (14 cm)

Sew charms and buttons onto C

Celebrate the seasons with Sunbonnet Sue! This miniature wall hanging features four unique scenes embellished with an appliquéd floral wreath.

SUNBONNET SUE MINI QUILT

MATERIALS

- Appliqué background fabric: Two fat eighths of print fabric
- Appliqué fabric: Assorted print scraps
- Patchwork fabric: Assorted print scraps
- Border fabric: ¾ yd (0.7 m) of green and white polka dot fabric
- Backing fabric: ¾ yd (0.7 m) of print fabric
- Binding fabric: ¼ yd (0.5 m) of print fabric
- Batting: 21¾ x 21¾ in (55 x 55 cm)
- 1¾ yds (1.5 m) of ¼ in (7 mm) wide rickrack
- #25 embroidery floss in green, light green, blue, pink, brown, yellow, and red

CUTTING INSTRUCTIONS

Trace and cut out the templates on Pattern Sheet D. Use the templates to cut out the following pieces, adding ¼ in (6 mm) seam allowance.

APPLIQUÉ BACKGROUND FABRIC

- 4 appliqué backgrounds

Use the templates to cut out the following pieces, adding ⅛ in (3 mm) seam allowance.

APPLIQUÉ FABRIC

- 4 Sunbonnet Sue motifs
- 4 border appliqué motifs

Sew using ¼ in (6 mm) seam allowance, unless otherwise noted.

Cut out the following pieces, which do not have templates, according to the dimensions listed below (these include seam allowance):

PATCHWORK FABRIC

- Lattice pieces (cut 4): 1¾ x 6½ in (4.2 x 16.2 cm)
- Lattice center (cut 1): 1¾ in (4.2 cm) square

BORDER FABRIC

- Side borders (cut 2): 4 x 13½ in (10.2 x 34.2 cm)
- Top and bottom borders (cut 2): 4 x 20½ in (10.2 x 52.2 cm)

BINDING FABRIC

- Binding: 2½ yds (2.2 m) of 1½ in (3.5 cm) wide bias strips

CONSTRUCTION STEPS

1. Appliqué and embroider the four motifs to the background fabrics as noted on the templates.

2. Sew the blocks and lattice pieces together as shown in the diagram on page 127.

3. Sew the rickrack to each border, then appliqué as noted on the template.

4. Sew the side borders to the left and right edges of the pieced panel, then sew the top and bottom borders in place.

5. Layer the quilt top, batting, and backing. Quilt as noted in the diagram on page 127. Use the quilting template on Pattern Sheet D to quilt the lattice.

6. Bind the quilt.

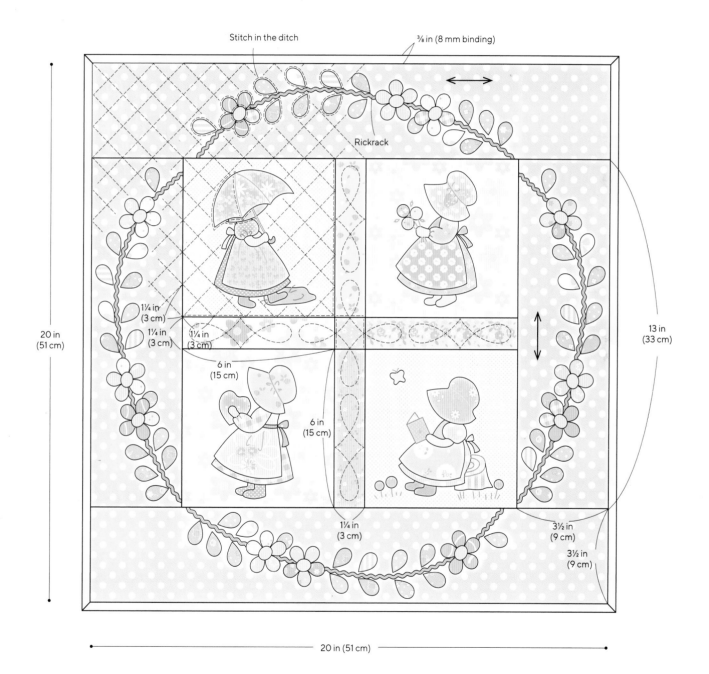

Stitch in the ditch

⅜ in (8 mm binding)

Rickrack

20 in (51 cm)

13 in (33 cm)

1¼ in (3 cm)

1¼ in (3 cm)

1¼ in (3 cm)

6 in (15 cm)

6 in (15 cm)

1¼ in (3 cm)

3½ in (9 cm)

3½ in (9 cm)

20 in (51 cm)

Pinch a rectangle of fabric into a tulip shape to make cute little ends for the drawstring cords.

Fussy cut sections of panel fabric to make these quick and easy drawstring pouches. Add a coordinating accent fabric for the casing and cord ends for a playful touch. These little bags work up quickly, so I like to make a few at once and have them on hand for gifts.

VINTAGE PANEL DRAWSTRING POUCHES

MATERIALS (FOR ONE POUCH)

- Pouch fabric: Two 9½ x 10¼ in (24 x 26 cm) fussy cut panels or fabric scraps
- Lining fabric: ½ yd (0.5 m) of print fabric
- 43¼ in (110 cm) of ⅛ in (3 mm) thick waxed cord

PROJECT DIAGRAM

POUCH (CUT 2)

10¼ in
(26 cm)

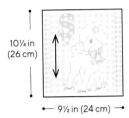

9½ in (24 cm)

LINING (CUT 1)

28¾ in
(73 cm)

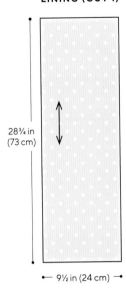

9½ in (24 cm)

CORD ENDS (CUT 2)

2¾ in
(7 cm)

4¼ in
(11 cm)

CUTTING INSTRUCTIONS

Cut out the following pieces, which do not have templates, according to the dimensions listed below (these include seam allowance):

POUCH FABRIC
- Pouch pieces (cut 2): 9½ x 10¼ in (24 x 26 cm)

LINING FABRIC
- Lining (cut 1): 9½ x 28¾ in (24 x 73 cm)
- Cord ends (cut 2): 4¼ x 2¾ in (11 x 7 cm)

CONSTRUCTION STEPS

1. Align the two pouch pieces with right sides together and sew along the bottom.

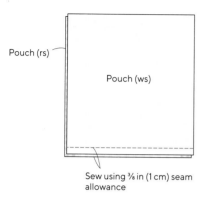

2. With right sides together, sew the lining to the two top edges of the pouch.

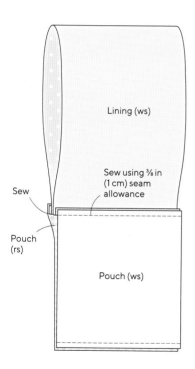

3. With right sides together, sew the two pouch pieces together along the sides. With right sides together, sew the lining together along one side, stopping ¾ in (2 cm) from the end to create an opening for the drawstring. Repeat process on the other side of the lining, but this time, leave a 2 in (5 cm) opening as well.

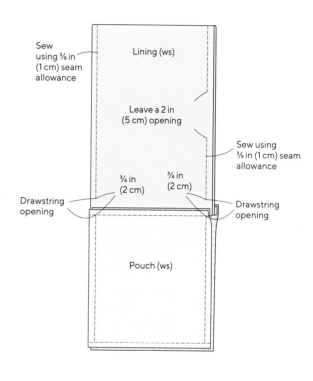

4. Turn right side out. Fold the lining opening seam allowances in and hand stitch closed. Do not stitch the drawstring openings closed.

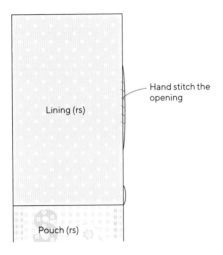

Hand stitch the opening

Lining (rs)

Pouch (rs)

5. Insert the lining into the pouch (the lining will extend higher than the pouch). Topstitch as shown in the diagram below to create a casing for the drawstring.

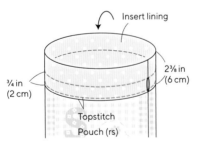

Insert lining

2⅜ in (6 cm)

¾ in (2 cm)

Topstitch

Pouch (rs)

6. Cut the waxed cord in half. Insert each cord through the casing in opposite directions. Sew the ends of each set together.

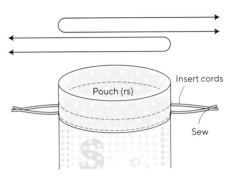

Insert cords

Pouch (rs)

Sew

7. Make the cord ends as shown below.

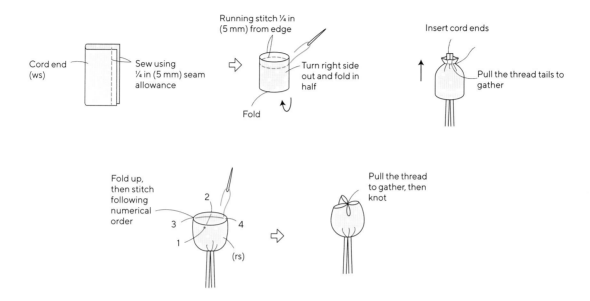

Cord end (ws)

Sew using ¼ in (5 mm) seam allowance

Running stitch ¼ in (5 mm) from edge

Turn right side out and fold in half

Fold

Insert cord ends

Pull the thread tails to gather

Fold up, then stitch following numerical order

Pull the thread to gather, then knot

FINISHED DIAGRAM

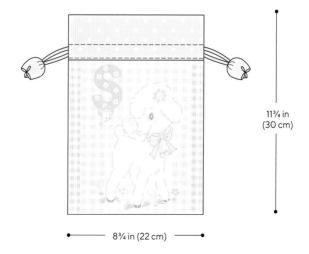

11¾ in (30 cm)

8¾ in (22 cm)

Use a printed panel fabric to whip up a baby gift in no time. This vintage-inspired panel even includes a lattice and borders, so all you have to do is add some quilting and bind the edges.

VINTAGE PANEL PLAYMAT

MATERIALS

- Top fabric: 43¼ x 39½ in (110 x 100 cm) of panel fabric
- Backing fabric: 43¼ x 39½ in (110 x 100 cm) of print fabric
- Batting: 47¼ x 43¼ in (120 x 110 cm)
- Binding fabric: ½ yd (0.5 m) of print fabric

CUTTING INSTRUCTIONS

Cut out the following pieces, which do not have templates, according to the dimensions listed below (these include seam allowance):

BINDING FABRIC
- Binding: 4½ yds (4 m) of 1½ in (3.5 cm) wide bias strips

Sew using
¼ in (6 mm) seam
allowance, unless
otherwise noted.

CONSTRUCTION STEPS

1. Layer the quilt top, batting, and backing. Quilt following the pattern of the fabric (refer to the photo below for an example of how to quilt this particular fabric).

2. Bind the quilt.

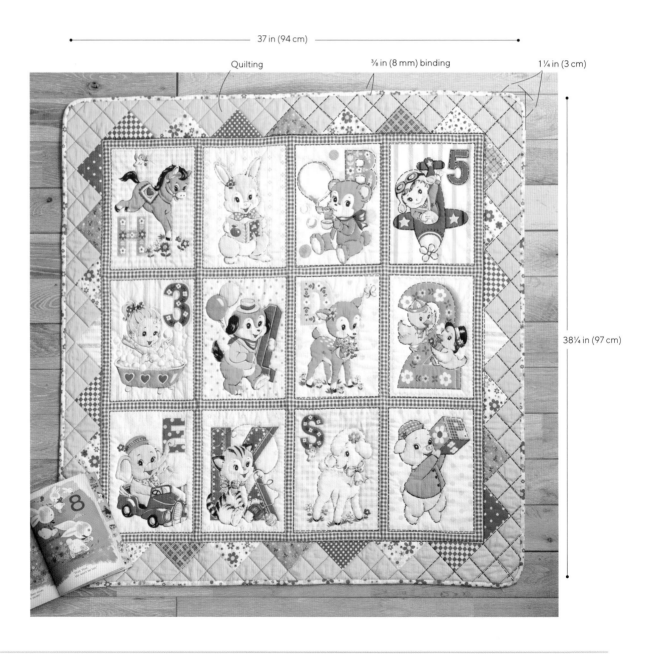

37 in (94 cm)

Quilting

⅜ in (8 mm) binding

1¼ in (3 cm)

38¼ in (97 cm)

BASIC QUILTING TECHNIQUES

This section includes general quilting techniques that you'll find helpful for constructing the projects in this book.

PATCHWORK

HOW TO MAKE TEMPLATES

Photocopy or trace the template from the pattern sheet. You can use paper templates or create more durable ones from card stock. To do this, tape the photocopy to a piece of card stock. Mark the corners by using a stiletto to punch holes in the card stock. Connect the marks with a ruler, then cut out the card stock template.

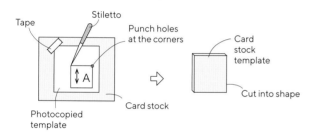

HOW TO CUT FABRIC

Align your fabric on your work surface with the wrong side facing up. Trace around your template. Make sure to leave space between each piece when tracing multiple pieces. Use a ruler to draw ¼ in (6 mm) seam allowance around each piece. Cut the pieces out along the seam allowance lines.

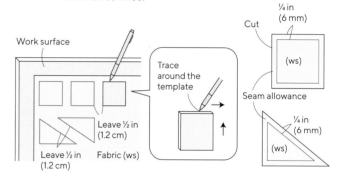

HOW TO HAND PIECE

Squares & Rectangles

Align two pieces of fabric with right sides together. Insert a pin at each seam allowance (① and ②) and then at the center (③). Thread a needle with one 16 in (40 cm) long strand of thread. Insert your needle in the seam allowance, about ⅛ in (3-4 mm) away from ①. Make one backstitch, then running stitch to ②. Make another backstitch in the seam allowance, then knot. Iron or finger press the seam toward the darker fabric.

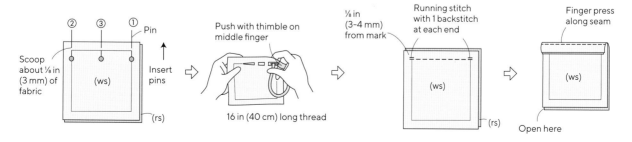

Rows

Prior to sewing rows together, you'll want to press the piece seam allowances in opposite directions for each row. This will ensure that the fabric lies flat and will prevent your quilt top from becoming bulky.

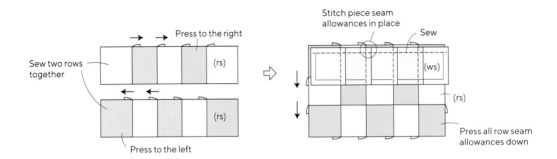

Hexagons

Align two hexagons with right sides together. Sew along one edge, starting and stopping one stitch in from the seam allowance mark. Align the next hexagon and sew from ★ to ★, then from ♡ to ♡. By avoiding the seam allowance, you'll create inset seams.

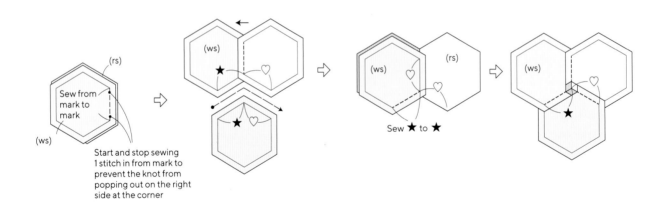

Triangles

Trim the corner seam allowances as shown below prior to sewing.

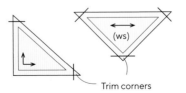

APPLIQUÉ

BASIC APPLIQUÉ

1. Align the background fabric on top of the template. Trace the appliqué design onto the right side of the background fabric. You may need to use a lightbox. Next, trace the appliqué design onto appliqué paper. Cut the design out, then adhere to the right side of the appliqué fabric.

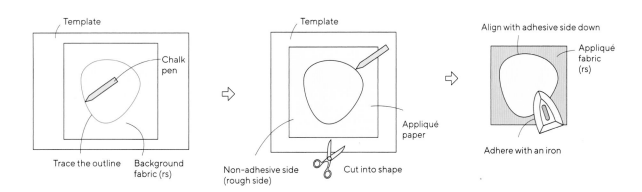

2. Add the seam allowance, then trim the appliqué fabric into shape. Apply a bit of glue to the wrong side of the appliqué fabric, then adhere it to the background fabric. Use the tip of the needle to fold the seam allowance under using the appliqué paper as a guide. Hand stitch the appliqué fabric to the background fabric using small vertical stitches. Remove the appliqué paper before you finish sewing the appliqué fabric in place.

Note: In this book, all appliqué pieces are cut out with a slightly smaller seam allowance than patchwork pieces. Use ⅛ in (3 mm) seam allowance for appliqué, unless otherwise noted.

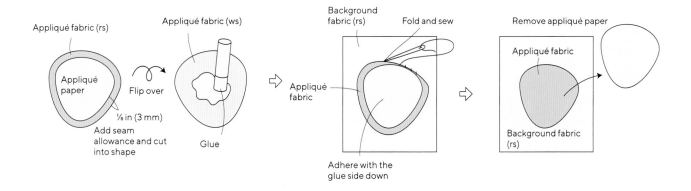

OVERLAPPED APPLIQUÉ

Some projects feature appliqué motifs where elements of the design overlap. When this is the case, mark the overlapped areas with a ★. When cutting out your appliqué fabric, add ¼ in (6 mm) seam allowance to these edges. As usual, add ⅛ in (3 mm) seam allowance to all other edges. When stitching the appliqué pieces in place, always start with the bottom layer of the design. If an area is going to be overlapped by another piece of appliqué fabric (as noted by ★), roughly hand baste it in place rather than finishing the edge. This will prevent the appliqué from becoming bulky.

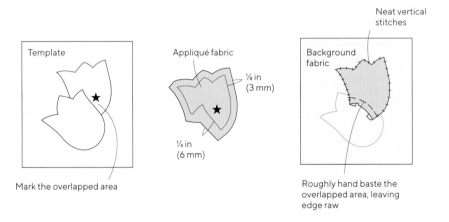

Template

Mark the overlapped area

Appliqué fabric

⅛ in (3 mm)

¼ in (6 mm)

Neat vertical stitches

Background fabric

Roughly hand baste the overlapped area, leaving edge raw

CORNERS & POINTS

Make small clips into the seam allowances of interior corners or sharp points. Use the tip of the needle to fold the seam allowance under. Make two overlapping stitches to secure these delicate areas in place.

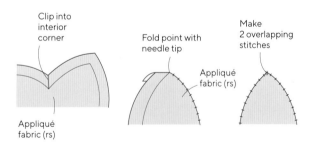

Clip into interior corner

Appliqué fabric (rs)

Fold point with needle tip

Appliqué fabric (rs)

Make 2 overlapping stitches

LONG, THIN APPLIQUÉS

Use a bias tape maker that can accommodate both a bias strip and fusible web tape. Remove the release paper backing from the fusible web and adhere the appliqué to the background fabric.

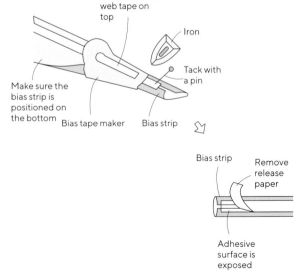

Position fusible web tape on top

Iron

Tack with a pin

Make sure the bias strip is positioned on the bottom

Bias tape maker

Bias strip

Bias strip

Remove release paper

Adhesive surface is exposed

QUILTING

MARK THE QUILTING LINES

Use a fabric pencil and ruler to draw quilting lines on the right side of your quilt top. Make light marks and be careful not to stretch the fabric.

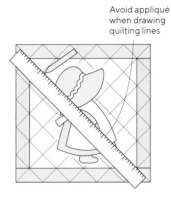

Avoid appliqué when drawing quilting lines

BASTE

Layer the quilt top, batting, and backing. Use basting thread to temporarily hold the three layers together with large stitches. Stitch a large cross shape, starting from the center and working toward the outside. Fill each quarter with parallel rows, about 1¼-1½ in (3-4 cm) apart.

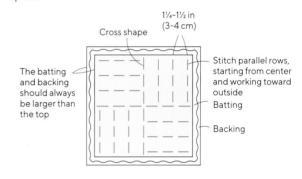

1¼-1½ in (3-4 cm)

Cross shape

The batting and backing should always be larger than the top

Stitch parallel rows, starting from center and working toward outside

Batting

Backing

HAND QUILTING

Quilt using one strand of thread in a coordinating color to the fabric. You'll use a rocking motion to push the needle through all three layers of the quilt and work the running stitch. Many of the projects in this book require you to "stitch in the ditch" which means you'll stitch right in the seam of the patchwork pieces or appliqué motif. You'll also find that many projects are quilted with intersecting diagonal lines which form a diamond shape. Once the quilting is complete, remove the basting stitches.

Side View of Quilting

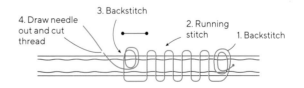

4. Draw needle out and cut thread

3. Backstitch

2. Running stitch

1. Backstitch

How to Start

To start stitching, make a knot at the end of the thread. Insert the needle through the right side of the quilt top, about ¾ in (2 cm) away from the starting point. Draw the needle out on the right side at the starting point. Pull the thread taut to draw the knot through the quilt top so it is hidden in the batting.

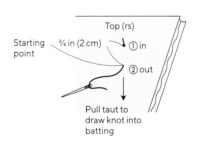

Top (rs)

Starting point

¾ in (2 cm)

① in

② out

Pull taut to draw knot into batting

How to Quilt

Place metal thimbles on the middle fingers of each hand. Use one thimble to push the needle through the layers of the quilt. Use the other thimble to receive the needle, then use the corner to push the needle tip back up through the layers of the quilt. Use a rocking motion to repeat this process to make 4-5 stitches that are even in length and spacing. Draw the needle out and pull the stitches taut. Continue quilting in this manner.

How to Finish

To finish stitching, make two backstitches in the same spot to prevent the thread from becoming loose. Draw the needle out on the right side of the quilt top a short distance away. Pull the thread taut and cut. The thread end will be hidden in the batting.

1 out
5 out 2 in
3 out 4 in

Pull thread taut then cut

How to Quilt with a Hoop

For large projects such as bags and quilts, use a hoop to hand quilt small sections at a time. Set the fabric into the hoop loosely so that the fabric has a little give to it. Use your body to push the hoop against the edge of your table or desk.

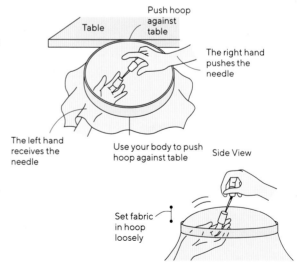

BINDING

Use fabrics strips cut on the bias, or diagonal, to finish the edges of your quilts. The following guide shows how to cut bias strips, sew them together, and then bind the edges of the quilt.

Note: This book uses ⅜ in (8 mm) finished binding for the majority of projects. This means that you'll need to cut 1½ in (3.5 cm) wide binding strips (this measurement includes seam allowance).

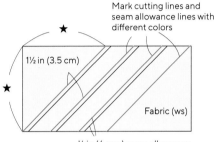

★ = Equal distance

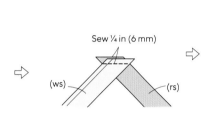

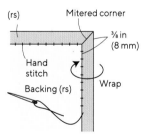

1. Mark your fabric with 45 degree parallel lines spaced 1½ in (3.5 cm) apart. Cut into strips.

2. Align two bias strips with right sides together and sew using ¼ in (6 mm) seam allowance. Continue sewing strips together until binding reaches desired length.

3. Fold the short end of the binding over ¼ in (6 mm). With right sides together, align the binding with the quilt, starting a short distance away from the corner. Sew until you reach the corner seam allowance.

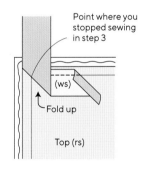

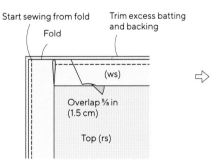

4. Fold the binding up and away from the quilt at a 45 degree angle.

5. Fold the binding back down, making a horizontal fold that aligns with the raw edge of the quilt. Continue sewing to attach the rest of the binding to the quilt using the same process at each corner. When you reach the end, overlap the two short ends ⅝ in (1.5 cm).

6. Wrap the binding around the raw edges of the quilt, mitering the corners. Fold the raw edge of the binding under and hand stitch to the backing.

STITCH GUIDE

HAND STITCHES

Ladder Stitch

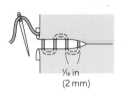

1/16 in
(2 mm)

Whipstitch

1/16- 1/8 in (2-3 mm)

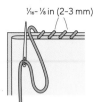

Blind Stitch

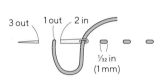

3 out   1 out   2 in

1/32 in
(1 mm)

Catch Stitch

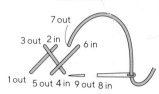

7 out
3 out 2 in   6 in
1 out 5 out 4 in 9 out 8 in

EMBROIDERY STITCHES

Outline Stitch

3   2
1

Blanket Stitch

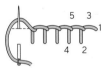

5   3
1
4   2

Feather Stitch

Straight Stitch

1   2
3   4
5

Herringbone Stitch

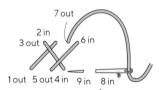

7 out
2 in
3 out   6 in
1 out 5 out 4 in   9 in   8 in

French Knot

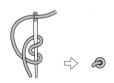

Lazy Daisy Stitch

Satin Stitch

Cross-Stitch

Note: Use #25 embroidery floss, unless otherwise noted.